Forever
MAX

Forever
MAX

The Lasting Adventures of the
World's Most Loved Dog

KERRY IRVING

with Matt Whyman

HARPER
element

HarperElement
An imprint of HarperCollins*Publishers*
1 London Bridge Street
London SE1 9GF

www.harpercollins.co.uk

HarperCollins*Publishers*
Macken House, 39/40 Mayor Street Upper
Dublin 1, D01 C9W8, Ireland

First published by HarperElement 2024

10 9 8 7 6 5 4 3 2 1

A catalogue record of this book is available from the British Library

ISBN 978-0-00-864504-5

Printed and bound in the UK using 100% renewable electricity at CPI Group (UK) Ltd

MIX
Paper | Supporting
responsible forestry
FSC
www.fsc.org
FSC™ C007454

This book is produced from independently certified FSC™ paper to ensure responsible forest management.

For more information visit: www.harpercollins.co.uk/green

I felt pain and loss and in need of care, I reached down for you, but you weren't there.

CONTENTS

PROLOGUE

'*Thank you, Max. For everything.*'

Right now, there is nowhere else that we would rather be. I've just found a nice place to settle on the floor of a glade. As I did so, my old dog came to rest in my lap. Manesty Woods has always been a favourite place of ours; a pocket of solitude in the valley of Borrowdale. It's a small, peaceful place on the southernmost shores of Derwentwater. From here, we can look across the water to the mighty slopes of Bleaberry Fell and Walla Crag. Sunlight fans through this opening in the tree canopy, illuminating the carpet of old, fallen leaves and the young ferns as they begin to unfurl for the season.

It's a time of renewal, but also one of reflection.

We're not alone here. Paddy and Harry are busy exploring the pathways and the rabbit holes hidden in the undergrowth. They've accompanied Max to the water's edge, but that's enough for him now. There was a time when he would splash and bound around just like the other two, brimming with energy and enthusiasm for

1

everything, but age catches up with us all. I comb my hand through his coat, aware of the warmth within. In so many ways, I've always taken comfort from that feeling. Even when life has seemed so cold and bleak, my loyal and loving friend has been there for me.

And now, as Max sighs and closes his eyes, I must be here for him.

'What a life, eh?' I say. 'And what a story we can tell.'

Part One

1

'If You Ever Want to Get Away From It All, Just Let Me Know'

NOT MANY SPRINGER SPANIELS CAN claim to have visited Buckingham Palace. When Max and I first met, years earlier at a challenging time in both of our lives, we could never have imagined that our story would take us to an audience with a future king and queen. Then again, when I first befriended that lonely little dog shut away in a yard, I couldn't see beyond the next day.

Our tale is one of companionship and of the healing power of loyalty and love. Max saved me from a crippling depression. At the time, I felt as if I had no future. Years later, when we accepted the invitation to the Royal Garden Party, we had raised £90,000 for charities such as the People's Dispensary for Sick Animals (PDSA). For his fundraising efforts, Max had even been honoured with a prestigious commendation award by them. That's what earned him an audience with William and Catherine on the cusp of summer 2019. Together with my wife, Angela, we travelled down to London by train from our home in the Lake District for a trip we would never forget. Standing in the palace grounds, mingling with invited guests from all walks of life, I felt so proud of everything Max had achieved. Above all, I hoped we had showed countless people around the world that life is worth living.

'What an honour that was!' I said to Angela on our return, having reunited with Paddy and Harry; two younger but just as big-hearted Springers that followed Max into our household in the years after he joined us. 'A once-in-a-lifetime experience.'

As it turned out, I was wrong. When it comes to a dog like Max, people from all walks of life see something in his soulful gaze that brings them back to him.

*　　*　　*

We live in Keswick, a traditional market town in the heart of the Lake District. Surrounded by hills and mountain peaks, with all kinds of weather in one day, it can be easy to forget about the wider world. With a love of the outdoors, we enjoy a simple and fulfilling life. As a result, it took us some time to recover from our adventure to London's hustle and bustle. Having been swept up in the excitement of the Royal Garden Party, we were quite happy to return to our little routines. Angela is a hairdresser, working from home, while I run a locksmith business. That means spending a lot of time in my van, driving to call-outs from shepherd's huts to stately homes, with the notorious Brown-Legged Gang riding alongside me.

When I started out, Max was my head of security. He travelled everywhere with me and became a familiar face across the fells. From the moment I adopted him, back in 2009, we had become inseparable. With a liver and white coat, a tail that didn't stop wagging and ears that flapped whenever the wind got up, Max had an uncanny empathy with people. He understood how they were feeling and responded accordingly. If I found myself becoming tense in traffic, a paw on my knee would calm me down. He gave me a reason to get outdoors, to remind myself what a wonderful world we have on our doorsteps, and I treasured our bond.

In 2017, Paddy rolled into our lives. A playful pup that liked nothing better than swinging from poor Max's ears, he effectively became the apprentice when it came to helping people and then shone in his own right. Paddy is a lovely, confident dog, who walks with quite a swagger. Unlike the rest of us, he's such a dude! Then there's dear Harry. He joined us when Paddy was just over a year old and had to find his place between two big personalities. While Paddy was in the springtime of his life, Max had reached the autumn of his years and sometimes needed someone to lean on. Harry came into his own here and would happily let Max rest against him whenever he needed. All three dogs went everywhere with me. In between jobs, we'd take off for wonderful walks around the lakes, through the valleys and over the hills, and that suited us just fine.

So, when I received a call a few weeks after our trip to Buckingham Palace, asking if I'd like to bring Max, Paddy and Harry to an upcoming event in town, I politely declined. Every year, we stage several charity walks in the Lake District. Like Max and Paddy, even Harry was learning to become an accomplished fund-raiser. They were recognised everywhere they went. With their welfare in mind, and because frankly I was still tired from the visit to London, I apologised to the nice, well-spoken lady who had rung me and hoped she'd understand.

'But we're celebrating the work of charities in the community,' she pressed on. 'We'd love you to come along with the dogs and share our special day.'

Patiently, I explained that although we raised funds for good causes, we weren't a charity.

'I'm sure there are plenty of organisations out there who do great things,' I said, really hoping she'd accept that it wasn't for us. 'It's such a giving town, you'll be spoiled for choice!'

The pause on the line told me she was about to play her ace card.

'But it's going to be in the main square,' she said. 'With a buffet!'

Now, the dogs like a free meal as much as I do, but this conversation was just reminding me how tired I still felt. The thought of being around yet more people was draining.

'Actually, I think we're busy that day,' I said weakly when she told me the date.

'Mr Irving, you will be coming,' she said and this time her tone had hardened considerably. 'Your invitation is already in the post. We look forward to your RSVP.'

It was, quite frankly, the strangest of calls. I rested my phone on the kitchen table and looked at the dogs: they seemed none the wiser.

'Who was that?' asked Angela.

'A very persuasive lady,' I said and shared the exchange I'd just had.

'At least you'll be fed.' Angela had popped down from her home salon upstairs. She was self-employed and rarely took time off, which left me wondering whether perhaps I should book a surprise holiday for her the week of the event. 'And it's a buffet – you're partial to a buffet.'

*   *   *

When my mobile rang for a second time, I worried it would be the same caller.

'Should I answer?' I asked out loud.

Max, Paddy and Harry were all looking at the phone. With some trepidation, I picked up and then breathed out long and hard when a friend introduced herself. A news photographer from the south of England, she was calling to ask if I could recommend a good holiday let in town for herself and the family.

'It's a working break,' she told me. 'I've heard that William and Kate will be making an official visit to Keswick. The Royal Family don't usually make a formal announcement about this kind of thing too early for security reasons, but word always gets out in media circles. I thought I'd find some accommodation before it all gets booked up because I'm hoping to get some pictures.'

'What date are they due to visit?' I asked.

My friend repeated the same one as the lady who had called me just minutes before. I gave Max the side eye. He'd retreated to his bed. Lying with his chin on his front paws, my spaniel returned the look.

He *knew*.

*　　　*　　　*

When the invitation arrived, a few days later, it made no mention of royal guests. Even so, Angela had persuaded me that I should attend. This time, the buffet wasn't a consideration. The Prince and Princess of Wales (known at the time as The Duke and Duchess of Cambridge) had only recently invited us to their place. It would seem rude for me to be absent when they visited mine. The only hitch was that one name was missing from the card: Max, Paddy, Harry and I were listed, but not Angela. So, now it was my turn to call the lady and refuse to take no for an answer.

'I'm sure my wife would love to meet the Cambridges again,' I said, hoping my loaded phrasing carried enough weight to persuade her. 'She got along so well with them last time.'

'Mr Irving, I don't know where your information is coming from,' she said and then cleared her throat as if that might stop her sounding so flustered, 'but let's just say even if Their Royal Highnesses were to attend, we simply don't have enough space.'

I tried again, but her response made it quite clear that she would not be negotiating. The invitation was extended to me and my dogs, she finished, while Angela could watch from the crowd if she wished to be there.

* * *

I was reluctant to go without Angela. Together with Max, Paddy and Harry, we're a team. If royalty were paying a visit, and they'd requested my attendance, I couldn't leave her out of it.

'Kerry, you have to be there,' she insisted. 'A royal tour of Keswick without Max just wouldn't be the same.'

'But, Ange, I know how much it would mean to you.'

'Do it for the dogs and for everyone that will come out to see them, including me.'

* * *

By the time the day arrived when Keswick was due to celebrate the community's charitable achievements, everyone was wise to the fact that it would be a royal visit. Even before the official announcement was made, an uncanny outbreak of patriotism had swept through our market town with bunting and flags in abundance.

That morning, thousands upon thousands of people flocked to the high street. Market days are always busy and bustling. This time, metal barriers kept the crowds back from the cobblestones. A huge gazebo stood at the top of the street under the town's famous Moot Hall's clock tower, as did plenty of burly, smartly dressed individuals who clearly served as bodyguards.

'Our head of security seems happy with arrangements,' I said to Angela, gesturing towards Max, who had settled for a snooze at my feet. He looked great in his signature orange coat, with Paddy and Harry in green and red respectively. 'I expect the other two will just want to know if snacks will be served.'

I had received instructions from the organisers to be at this spot with the dogs at precisely quarter past ten. The plan was for the royal couple to arrive at the gazebo and then tour the charities, who had set up their stalls along the high street. I had been advised that I should dress normally, which came as a relief – I'd worn a suit as required for the garden party, but it just wasn't me. Even so, as I'd spent more time making sure the boys looked smart in their colourful coats, Angela checked that my shirt was at least tucked in properly for this second royal audience. She also accompanied us into town, which left me feeling so torn. Although she kept saying how happy she was to be watching from behind the barrier, it still didn't feel right.

'You'll be OK by yourself, you have the boys,' she said brightly. 'Let them do the talking.'

I knew what she meant. Max, Paddy and Harry always helped me to settle into social situations. Dogs make terrific ice-breakers. I can stand behind them knowing they'll be the focus of any conversation I may have. It takes away so much anxiety and really helped when a lady from the council left the gazebo and strode towards me. She had a clipboard, which she consulted before finding what she was looking for and adding a tick.

'Mr Irving, we would like you and the dogs to stand over there.' She took two steps back as she said this, turned and pointed to a precise spot under the gazebo. 'And don't move.'

I swapped a wary glance with Angela and then slipped through a gap in the barriers with Max, Paddy and Harry so we could do as we had been told. Once we were in position, the woman switched back to pick out other guests, tick them off her list and direct them to their designated spots under the canvas. I just clutched the ends of three leads, comforted by the fact that I was here with my three best friends. I could sense people from the crowd looking at me and the dogs, but if Max, Paddy and Harry sensed it too then they remained completely relaxed. Even when cheering rose up from somewhere behind the hall, marking the moment that the royal couple arrived, they stayed right by my side.

'Remember to bow,' I told Paddy as I stood up straight and told myself to breathe calmly and slowly.

By now, the number of people invited to stand under the gazebo, along with security, media crews and photographers, made it quite hard for me to see the arrival of the two very special guests. As I was straining to get a glimpse, a member of the Palace party politely asked me for a quick word.

'I don't want to sound funny,' he said, 'but we'd like you and the dogs to step outside.'

'Really?' I said in surprise, pressing my hands to my chest. 'I've showered.'

He smiled in a slightly pained way and invited me to follow him into the sunshine. From behind the barrier, I could see Angela looking at me with some concern. I figured there had been some huge mix-up, until his formal manner softened.

'I was involved in arranging your visit to Buckingham Palace,' he said. 'The pictures of Max with William and Catherine were a big hit but what the press want today is a shot of the royal couple with *all* the dogs.'

'Oh,' I said, feeling like I was a second behind what was going on. 'Do you need me in the frame, too?'

'Of course.' We stopped midway across the cobbles between the gazebo and the crowds. He looked around, seemingly puzzled. 'Where is your lovely wife? She was with you for the Garden Party.'

'She wasn't invited,' I explained. 'I did try.'

The man from the Palace looked horrified.

'Oh no, no, no, we can't have that! Is she here this morning?'

'Over there,' I said. 'Behind you.'

The man wheeled around. Following a click of his fingers, summoning his people to escort her, Angela was back at my side. Within a blink, so too was the lady from the council with her clipboard. This time, she brought a stern glare with her, drew breath to no doubt inform my wife that she had no right to be here, only for our new friend to come to our rescue once more.

'Mrs Irving is here by *special* request,' said the man from the Palace, upon which the poor woman shrank to about half her size. 'The Cambridges have specifically asked to meet the couple and their dogs.'

Once again, this day was shaping up to be as memorable as our visit to the Palace.

*　　*　　*

By now, the royal couple were circulating among guests under the gazebo. Dressed in a smart utility jacket, belted at the waist, with black jeans and boots, Catherine's casual look helped to put everyone at their ease. William wore a suit with a shirt open at the neck and displayed the same easy charm as he had at our first introduction. The crowd behind us looked on with great excitement, with many recording the moment on their phones. I was excited, but also very nervous – I wished I could be as relaxed as Harry. The sun was shining brightly that morning and he had taken full advantage by lying down to bask on the warm cobblestones. Meanwhile, both Max and Paddy joined Angela and me in waiting for our big moment to come.

'Stand to attention, Harry,' I whispered when the royal couple emerged into the sunshine. 'Look who it is!'

My young spaniel didn't even twitch. For a heartbeat, I was horrified. Then I glanced at Angela and reminded myself that young dogs were a law unto themselves.

'Let him be,' she said as we both prepared to be introduced to Their Royal Highnesses for the second time in a matter of weeks.

*   *   *

The next few minutes felt like a dream, just as they had at the Palace. Both William and Catherine made a fuss of Max, who responded like he was in the company of old friends, while the press got their picture of Paddy gazing up warmly at the Duchess as she stroked his ear. It captures a wonderful moment. Both Angela and I felt so privileged to catch up with the royal couple once again and to talk about their dogs and the love they have for them. It doesn't matter whether you're a prince or a pauper, it seems, our four-legged friends bring everyone together.

Throughout our conversation, the people in charge of the visit looked on as if they had timed this exchange to the nanosecond. William and Catherine had a packed itinerary ahead of them, with thousands of people hoping to engage with them in some way across the course of a long day and I couldn't help but think what a huge responsibility that must be. As our conversation turned from dogs to the walking events we hosted to raise money for good causes and then the sheer pleasure of rambling in the Lakes, I suddenly found myself extending a friendly invitation that no doubt caused the lady with the clipboard to wish she'd phoned in sick.

'If you ever want to get away from it all,' I said, 'just let me know. Give me a shout. We'll take you out onto the fells.'

It slipped out from nowhere, as if I had momentarily forgotten I was in the presence of royalty. Even as I heard myself, sounding so casual as I addressed the royal couple, I worried I might be met by silence.

For a moment, William looked at me as if to process what I'd just said.

'Do you know what?' he said finally. 'I'd love that.'

Now, I knew it would never happen, but his reply was deeply heartfelt. As the royal couple's entourage encouraged them to move on towards the charity stands, pausing first to greet the crowds, I felt huge admiration for them both. Together, William and Catherine carry so much on their shoulders and dedicate their lives to the roles and responsibilities invested in their titles. Still, in that brief exchange I realised that for all their privilege it must be so hard to enjoy life's simple pleasures. I couldn't imagine how it must be if I was unable to just take off for a walk with my dogs. It meant so much to me, and in a very different way to the man who would be king.

2
Let the Dogs Do the Talking

THE EVENING AFTER THE ROYAL COUPLE came to town, Max, Paddy and Harry were back in the media once more. It wasn't just the local press but the national news, with the picture of Paddy looking up at Catherine becoming the shot that summed up the day. These three Springer Spaniels were stars on the rise and the peace and quiet we craved became a little further out of reach.

After our visit to Buckingham Palace, we were looking forward to returning to our ordinary lives. Now, in the wake of a second encounter with William and Catherine, it felt like the spotlight was shining even more brightly upon us. Our Facebook community page – which is such a lovely, kind and supportive place – had always grown at a steady rate. It's where people come to catch up with our adventures across the Lake District, make friends and even join in on our charity walks in person or by connecting virtually from anywhere around the world.

Following our double brush with royalty and the public attention this brought us, the numbers simply soared. With coverage in everything from *Hello!* magazine to the American fashion bible, *Harper's Bazaar*, we reached 100,000 followers. What's more, that number continued to rise, as did the positive feedback from those who saw something special in the dogs. I was hugely proud of Max, Paddy and Harry for bringing so much to people's lives. It's just in the back of my mind a small voice kept reminding me not to neglect my own welfare. Over a decade earlier, stress, anxiety and depression had nearly killed me. Without Max to lead me from that dark and lonely place, joined later by Paddy and Harry to become an inseparable band of brothers, I wouldn't be here today.

With attention rising, I felt somewhat torn. I knew how much the dogs meant to people and so many were facing challenges of their own. It was touching to hear from members of the community who were dealing with anything from health to personal, relationship or financial issues – and causing no end of stress and worry – to say they felt a connection with these three spaniels. They had become a lifeline in some ways, particularly to those who were housebound or just sought a ray of light from the dark place in which they found themselves. A clip of Max, Harry and Paddy at play on the fells provided a small pleasure to people around the world and this in turn inspired me. I loved uploading little moments from our walks along tracks or through woods and open fells, or capturing them snoring on the sofa at the end of a long day. As much as I felt rewarded in knowing what sharing our lives online meant to others, I was also mindful of the fact that at heart I'm quite a private person.

As someone who loved being alone with my dogs, just following a path to see where it led, I also found the upswing in public-speaking invitations to be somewhat overwhelming. On the one hand, I was deeply flattered that people wanted to hear about life with Max, Paddy and Harry, and the healing powers of canine companionship. If that helped just one person in the audience then it had to be worthwhile. On the other, it meant standing on a stage feeling far from my comfort zone.

Fortunately, I was never alone.

*   *   *

'This morning, boys, we're back to school. Best behaviour, OK?'

Talking to teenagers can be great fun, but I also find it slightly stressful. They can have a low tolerance to any talk that fails to hit the mark and so I am always braced for mine to fall apart within minutes. On a typical visit, such as the one that morning to a local secondary school, I had been asked to come in with Max, Paddy and Harry to focus on dogs and mental health. They always accompany me because frankly without them, I could never stand on that stage. It also helps that they're the main attraction – I'm just the guy who drives the van and gives a speech while everyone looks at them. It works out well that way. They may not say much but I'm happy to let my dogs do the talking.

In reception, we were met by the headmaster. He pumped my hand and then petted the dogs while telling me how much he enjoyed our community page. Then he asked how long my talk would last. When I suggested about sixty minutes the smile on his face looked like it had suddenly become uncomfortable to maintain.

'You've probably got about half an hour before they get restless,' he advised me. 'Is that OK?'

'Sure,' I said as he led the way to the school auditorium, while quietly hoping that Max, Paddy and Harry would weave their magic spell and effectively stop time so I could finish my planned speech.

At every school we visit, I find it's important to let the dogs settle into the space before the pupils come flooding in. They need to feel safe and secure, rather than suddenly finding themselves in a packed house full of excitable kids. With this in mind, we had arrived early, as planned. Inside the auditorium, I let them off their leads so they could explore and familiarise themselves. The seats were arranged in steep tiers, looking down at a stage bathed in spotlight. I sensed a knot tighten in my stomach and promptly reminded myself that I would not be alone.

By the time the year groups filed in, which amounted to about 300 kids, I was in position on the stage. While

Max sat quietly at my side, Harry had found a high-heeled shoe from an old theatre production. At least I hoped it was old because he was busy chewing it! Paddy was still coolly pacing the floor, looking like the star of the show, while I stood beside my laptop, which was plugged into an overhead projector. An image of the three boys on the fells filled the screen behind us. As the pupils took to their seats, not one of them made a sound. The sight of three dogs in school, plus a briefing from the teachers that everyone needed to be on their best behaviour so as not to startle them, saw every single boy and girl settle down in rapt silence. I looked to the floor and smiled to myself: if only their parents and carers could see them now.

'Well, hello everyone,' I began once every seat had filled, only to catch my breath as the image of the dogs disappeared from the screen and a ripple of laughter spread across the auditorium. I looked down at my laptop, just as the cable that Paddy had accidentally pulled out from its socket hit the floor. Even I couldn't help but chuckle as I restored the feed. Within seconds of opening my talk, everyone felt at ease and we had the dogs to thank for that.

Max, Paddy and Harry brought sunshine to the stage and yet the talk I went on to give explored a dark place in my past. Whereas I might focus on environmental issues at primary school visits and the importance of looking after our wonderful surroundings, I was purposely hard-hitting for this age group. Our mental health is such a precious thing and key to living a fulfilling life. So, I talked about how close I came to giving up, feeling housebound and helpless in the wake of a road accident that had left me in chronic pain. At that time, over ten years ago, I considered myself to be nothing but a burden to Angela. I'd lost sight of the fact that she loved me as much as I loved her. It was my wife who got me out of the house, in fact, after months in despair behind closed curtains. All she did was encourage me to pick up some milk from the corner shop and in that small errand, I happened to come across a lonely dog who sought the same reason for living as me.

By the time I reached the end of my talk, about an hour and a half had passed. In that time, with three Springers as a focal point, everyone had hung onto my every word. In some ways it's a simple story of a life-saving friendship between one man and his dogs, but I believe there's also a message in there that speaks to us all.

'Look after each other,' I said to finish. 'Together, we can only be stronger.'

Then, following a whole raft of questions – from *what car do you drive?* to *what's your net income after tax?* – I invited anyone who would like to meet Max, Paddy and Harry to come to the front. By now, thanks to their presence, the mood in the hall was calm and respectful. Of course, friends chatted to each other in low voices as a line began to form, but the teachers had no need to keep anyone in check. This was young people at their very best and it was all down to the dogs. As the pupils took turns to step up and say hello, with many crouching to stroke, pet and even talk to them, the headmaster appeared at my side.

'Some of these kids come from challenging backgrounds,' he said, having thanked me for our time. 'What's happening here is incredible, it's so inspiring.'

As I watched my boys greet one young person after another, giving each one the time to feel safe and special in their company, I felt so proud. They stole the show, as they did every time, and that was a job well done. Afterwards, having headed out to find a good stretch of the countryside for us to explore, I reflected on what this meant. Yes, I found these visits to be intense in terms of preparation and performance. Then again, if we could make a difference to just one young life then it had to be worthwhile.

*   *   *

As well as school visits, we also found ourselves invited to give the same talk in the workplace. The Lake District is home to several important power stations. They're located in remote places and can employ vast numbers of people. In some ways, on driving in through the main gates as a visitor, it can feel like arriving in a community cut off from the outside world.

25

It's the staff car parks that tell me a great deal. All the spaces are filled with really nice cars and gleaming motorbikes. The people are well paid here. They're on solid salaries with all the perks, yet in my view they seem economically trapped. Employment offering this kind of remuneration is scarce across the region and so choices are limited. Yes, they can support their families and go on nice holidays, but for some that can feel like a gilded cage. This isn't just my impression, I learned, but one often shared by my hosts. It's also the reason why they ask me to come in with the dogs and share my story.

As I talk about my experience, I can see faces in the audience almost looking inwardly. In the grip of depression, I locked myself away. I felt like I couldn't leave my own house or talk about the dark thoughts that occupied my mind. I didn't think anyone would understand, or want to listen, and even if they had, I would have struggled to find the right words. With Max at my side, I learned to find my own way back into the world. His companionship was key; my silent friend who was always there for me. That gave me the courage to find my feet once more and then my sense of purpose. From there, as a survivor in some ways, I came to recognise the value of reaching out whenever life gets tough even if it's just by spending time with a faithful four-legged friend.

There have been moments when members of the audience have stepped up in line to meet Max, Paddy and

Harry while furiously wiping tears from their cheeks. Some have even made a fuss of the dogs only to bury their faces into their coats and weep. It's almost always men, which tells me a great deal. Our mental health plays such a pivotal role in our lives, yet so many of us don't know how to reach out for support when we need it. Whenever I brought the boys in and shared my story, those barriers came down. Even if members of the audience dried their eyes after the event and returned to their posts, often working long shifts in isolation, I hoped it shows that help is always out there. People live tough lives, even though it may not seem that way from the outside. That always put things in perspective for me. As much as I valued time to myself, I always had my dogs. In that view, I was never alone. They weren't simply my constant companions, Max, Paddy and Harry were therapists who never had to say a word to help me. I could talk to them and find my own solutions, or just get out for a nice walk with them and find some much-needed perspective. I hoped that in sharing our experience on stage, we encouraged people to realise that help is always out there, no matter what their situation, and often from a source that might otherwise be overlooked.

3

A Moment to Ourselves

UNLIKE MAX, I HAVE NEVER BEEN a good sleeper. As the demands on our time grew, and I began to run on empty, I found myself turning in for bed quite early each evening. I could nod off quite quickly, especially after such long days, but ultimately my bad back would wake me early.

It's an old injury; the result of a minor traffic accident with major consequences. Nerve damage to my spine left me living with chronic pain, caused me to give up on my career in agricultural sales and led to my decline into depression. I'm much better now, thanks to my dogs for getting me out and about and restoring my mental health, but physically, it's still uncomfortable.

As a result, I would always be awake by half past four in the morning so rather than stare up at the ceiling or spend hours until daybreak trying to get comfortable, I would dress and pad downstairs to see my dogs.

'Good morning, boys,' I whispered one morning, on finding all three dogs with tails thumping against the interior of their baskets. They would always be awake at this time – for them, it was routine. Plus, they knew that it meant they were about to head out for a walk before Keswick rises.

A few months after the Royal visit, we had been invited to give a little presentation to a primary school in Whitehaven, a port on the Northwest Coast. The kids were so sweet. They were greatly concerned about our environment when I showed pictures of Max with a bandaged paw after he'd cut it on glass in the fells and a clip of Harry swimming in the lake with a plastic bottle in his mouth that he'd waded out to retrieve. What troubled me, however, was the fact that when I asked for a show of hands, none of them had visited the Lake District. It's literally on their doorstep, yet there are areas surrounding the Lakes that experience real poverty and deprivation.

Some of these kids, I learned, hadn't even been to the beach and that broke my heart. I'm a sensitive sort of person and still felt quite sad about it for some time afterwards. When I slipped out of the front door with the dogs the next day before dawn, I felt all the more grateful to Max for helping me to connect with the outside world.

'Nice and quiet now,' I reminded them as we made our way up the street. At such an early hour, I let my dogs roam off-lead. They never left my side, even if Paddy sometimes liked to strut ahead by a few metres.

We passed through pools of light from streetlamps while puddles from overnight rain seemed to trap stars from the sky overhead.

I loved this early walk before our day got underway. Whatever the weather, before my phone started filling with messages we would be up and out. It could feel like time had stopped for us and we were free to float towards the churchyard, down to the lake or across the park in blissful silence. It gave me time to think, reflect and make peace with the world. I still felt so sorry for those school kids, but at least I could remind myself that perhaps meeting Max, Paddy and Harry would encourage them to broaden their horizons. If not straight away, then at least as they found their feet with independence – they're our future, after all.

On that morning, as I did at the dawn of every day, I returned home with the dogs, feeling like a weight had lifted from my shoulders. A simple walk with my best friends, just as light warms the horizon, that's all it was and yet I could think of no better tonic in life.

It was still early, but I could rely on the dogs not to make too much noise because they always knew what was in store for them next. Even before I'd peeled off my coat, they would be waiting for me to take them into the kitchen for breakfast. There, three bowls awaited them. Springers can be somewhat excitable, especially when it comes to meal times, which is why it's so important to channel that into good behaviour.

'Steady now, Paddy. Your turn will come.'

When Max first came to live with us because his previous owner was moving on, he struck me as a dog with natural-born manners. That gentle spirit shone through in everything he did and began with sitting automatically for his bowl as I filled it at the counter. Paddy and then Harry were both pups when they joined the fold. Their enthusiasm for food used to make me laugh so much. Paddy in particular could bounce so high on his hind legs, but then I also loved working with them to recognise when it was time to be calm and show patience. I think they learned a lot from Max at mealtimes too because they quickly followed his example. Even when he played by the rules, Paddy could quiver in anticipation and then fall upon his food to inhale it and even my quieter Harry can also lose himself in a breakfast binge.

Almost always, both dogs would leave a few kibbles in their bowls or on the floor. There would be no need for me to clean up after them, however – I could leave that to Max, who always waited for my nod before he set to work. I didn't teach him such patience. It was just there in his heart; a dog who had spent his early years alone in a yard and never gave up hope that things would always get better.

I was immensely proud of all three dogs for bringing so much positivity into people's lives, but with that came responsibilities. Above all, it was important to me that everyone who joined our Facebook page felt recognised and welcome, which meant taking lots of photographs on our adventures out on the hills and sharing them regularly. I've always loved playing with the camera and so it never felt like work. Even so, it was one more thing to add to the mix in between work. When I first became a locksmith, which was a reinvention after the accident as I could no longer sit at a desk for long periods, I found I really enjoyed the job. I became my own boss and the dogs joined me in the van for the ride. Even so, when the Facebook community took off, I began to realise that what I looked forward to most was the time in between jobs. Walking with Max, Harry and Paddy meant so much to me. Once I recognised that their lives meant so much to others too, I started to think how we could turn that into a lasting force for good.

Which is how the charity walks had started.

For our first event, I wasn't sure if anyone would turn up. When about 100 people arrived, many with their dogs, we enjoyed a fantastic ramble around the shore of Derwentwater Lake. Not only did everyone have a great time, but we also raised a decent sum of money for local causes. This didn't just come from those who joined us for the walk. The online donations took my breath away. It also made me aware that with that came quite a responsibility: it meant making sure that everyone who joined us was safe and felt looked after. We also had to think about parking, as well as providing food and drink.

As each event grew bigger than the last, I was so grateful to a local café, The Lingholm Kitchen & Walled Garden, for accommodating us. We would start and finish there, and sit out in their beautiful walled garden when the weather allowed. It was good for their business and also allowed us to make a difference to the wider community. Those were happy days, which cost me nothing but time.

It's just time was becoming increasingly pressed.

Mostly this was down to numbers. Our charity walks went from around 100 people taking part to upwards of 1,000. To celebrate Max's birthday one year, we hosted an event called 'A Brew for Moo', which was my nickname for him. It meant finding a local farm that could accommodate everyone. On the day, it was such a joy to meet so many people from the Facebook community. Most strikingly of all, the donations came in from all over the world. What really hit home for me was the fact that as humans we want to help each other, even from afar. A walk with a dog beside us is a simple pleasure, but also priceless in terms of our health and happiness. Sadly, it's not something that's available to us all. We live in different lives and sometimes in circumstances that can leave us feeling like something is missing.

Aware that so many people in our community were drawn to supporting Max, Paddy and Harry as a way of involving dogs in their lives, I decided to give something back to them in return, which is where the calendars came in.

'Sorry about the boxes,' I said to Angela in the autumn of that year. 'It seemed like a good idea at the time.'

I was standing in the hallway when my wife ventured downstairs. Having just unloaded the van, following a collection run to the printer's, I suddenly felt quite ridiculous: this was our home after all and not a warehouse.

'That's a lot of calendars,' she said diplomatically, given that I had effectively halved the width of our hallway. 'But a lovely thing to do, Kerry.'

I opened a box to show her that year's edition. Like the charity walks, it had started as a small venture and grown into something far bigger than I could have imagined.

'Do you like it?' I asked hopefully.

Angela leafed through the calendar. I had taken all the photographs myself. Each month showed Max, Paddy and Harry at their best, which generally boiled down to looking like they were having the time of their lives around the Lakes.

'I don't like it,' she said, 'I *love* it! Just make sure they don't stay there for long.'

I didn't need to be told. With three active spaniels in the house, we needed all the space we could get. Besides, I really wanted to get the calendars to their rightful homes in time for Christmas. As always, it had been an absolute joy to put them together, from sorting through thousands of pictures for twelve that would make the cut and then doing everything from design to production myself. But as the venture grew bigger with every year, it put pressure on our everyday lives. Often, I'd find myself rushing to get home in the van after work so that I could deal with orders, or take time out so I could queue in the Post Office. I spent so much time there, in fact, that I became good friends with the postmaster. It helped that he really loved dogs because Max, Paddy and Harry never left my side. But now we were running out of space and time to make the most of everything. Without that early-morning walk, a moment to ourselves before the world woke up, we wouldn't have known where to begin ...

4

Kings of the Road

'GUYS? WHY ARE WE DOING THIS?'

I asked the question en route to a call-out. We were on our way to an address that had appointed me key holder. Most properties that I watched over as part of the package were stately homes open to the public. It meant they were left empty overnight or for long periods out of season. If a security alarm rang, or someone reported suspicious activity, I'd be summoned to investigate. Naturally, I always took my three trusty security guards along with me. Nine times out of ten, we'd discover a window that hadn't been properly shut and a breeze had triggered the alarm, or a cat had found its way in with the same outcome. That morning, having visited the property in question many times before, I knew full well it would be a false alarm, which is when I voiced my frustration to the dogs: 'It's a beautiful day. Is this really how we should be spending it?'

From the passenger seat, Max responded by looking at me side on and then turning to rest his chin in my lap.

I glanced in the rear-view mirror: Paddy and Harry were sitting in their baskets. Both had pricked up their ears.

'Sorry,' I said, sensing the stress I had felt suddenly ease now I had voiced it. 'I couldn't do any of this without you guys. I just wonder why we're doing it at all?'

The answer, of course, was because we needed to earn a living. Even so, as we followed a road under a majestic Cumbrian sky, I had questioned out loud if it was really worth it. You can chase money, but you can't chase time and that's what I valued more than anything else. Having suffered with my physical and mental health and come through determined not to take it for granted, there I was in a job that left me increasingly dissatisfied. Only the company of my dogs made it bearable. Without them, I worried that I'd find myself slipping back into the same dark place in my mind from where Max had first rescued me.

'You understand me,' I said, briefly resting one hand on his head and then smiling to myself when he sighed. 'I know, buddy.'

In my rear-view mirror, as we followed a lane banked by dry stone walls, I could see that Harry had ventured forward so he could peer over the three front seats at the road ahead. Paddy, meanwhile, had stationed himself at the back to check the way we'd come. It was something they always did. In that same moment, I was reminded how closely all three of them watched over me and I vowed to make more time for us all.

*   *   *

'I was thinking about a road trip,' I said to Angela that evening. We'd just finished washing up after supper and had settled in front of the wood burner in the front room. Max, Paddy and Harry had already flopped on the floor, strategically placing themselves for maximum heat absorption. They were busy quietly cooking themselves as they loved to do. 'We could take my work van,' I added.

My wife was looking at her phone. She had dropped it a few days earlier and cracked the screen. Judging by her frown, my suggestion had just caused the cracks to spread a little further.

'Kerry,' she said and set the phone in her lap, 'you know what I'm like about dog hair.'

I did. Whenever I gave Angela a lift, she'd spend a few minutes picking solitary strands off the passenger seat before climbing in.

'I'll get it valeted,' I said, which made her smile.

'Where did you have in mind for this road trip?' she asked.

As someone who loved being outdoors, I was always keen to explore the beautiful, rugged playground we called home. Every now and then, if it was a nice warm evening at the end of the week, I'd go further than just a late walk with the dogs. We'd jump in the van and drive to the back of the fells behind Keswick. It's no more than a mile or so from home, but strikingly remote. There, after a ramble along High Pike with the boys in the late sun, I would throw open the van's sliding door so we could watch the midges call it a night and the stars come out. Then, when the temperature cooled under moonlight, we'd close up the van and settle into a kind of makeshift sleepover. I'd share the same space as my three spaniels. Yes, they could be smelly and wriggled constantly, but I loved it. Apart from the very first time we took Harry. He only disappeared for a minute on our walk, but it became horrifyingly apparent when we were back in the van that he had spent it rolling in a dead sheep.

The smell had been so awful that even Max and Paddy looked like they were suffocating. With a head-torch on, I took that little spaniel across to a stream to wash him down, but by then the stench was in my nose and the van's upholstery. All I could do was lie down with the dogs in the back and hope that sleep would rescue me. It was dire and yet when we woke at dawn and let the fresh air in, I still didn't want to be anywhere else in the world.

This time, however, I wanted to expand our horizons.

'So, I was thinking about Scotland,' I said to Angela. 'For a couple of days. Maybe even a week?'

For some time, I'd had my eye on an epic loop around the North Highlands. Known as the NC500, this popular choice for cyclists and caravanners started and finished at Inverness. Designed to showcase Scotland at its finest, the North Coast 500 route took in castles, lochs and crags and effectively celebrated the open road. The moment I decided that we didn't have a moment more to waste with Max, it seemed like this was the ideal time.

'Well, that sounds lovely,' said Angela, smiling despite herself. 'Will there be a pool?'

I drew breath to be sure she had registered what kind of trip I had in mind here and then realised she was teasing me. The fact was that my wife could barely last more than a minute in the van before one of the dogs tried to settle on her lap. She loved them to bits, but there were limits.

'It's not your idea of a break, is it?' I said, feeling suddenly quite sheepish. I had become so caught up in the idea of just taking to the high road that I completely lost sight of what I was proposing here. 'It was a daft idea,' I added. 'Forget I even mentioned it.'

'Well, I think it's just what you need,' she said, which took me by surprise.

'Really?'

'I'd quite like the peace and quiet at home,' she told me. 'A dog-free holiday.'

Angela and I both liked our space. Sometimes we interpreted that in different ways, though we would always be able to count on each other when we needed it. Above all, she had stood by me when my life fell apart after the road accident. Without her encouragement, I'd never have left the house. Nor would I have met Max and for that, I will be forever grateful. Through my eyes, she will always be one of a kind.

'Are you sure?' I asked.

'Absolutely.' Angela clasped her phone once more, running a finger over the screen. 'You can call and tell me all about it at the end of each day … on my new phone.'

I realised I was about a heartbeat behind what was going on. I chuckled and told her that was just what I had in mind. We had a deal. Everyone was happy. Which is just how it should be.

*   *   *

September is a lovely month. It bridges two seasons. I love the late hazy sun that can mark those days as much as the freshening pinch in the air at night. As we crossed the border into Scotland, which is not far north from the Lakes, I wound down the front windows so the dogs could get a sniff of the journey we had in store.

'This is the life!' I declared, feeling suddenly free from the burden of work. I'd left a message on my answer machine, created an out-of-office email and basically closed the business for five days. I'd be back, I promised my clients, and privately I hoped that I would do so with a renewed passion for my profession. 'This is what it's all about!'

Until my return, I didn't care about keys or locks. I was free to enjoy life with my dogs. We were on our way to Inverness, heading in an anticlockwise direction. Why? Because I wanted to save the West Coast until last. I'd once taken Max to a spot south of Mallaig, along the famous Road to the Isles. There, we had walked across a beach with bone-white sand and not a soul in sight. Now I wanted to share that with Paddy and Harry. I couldn't say how long it would take us to get there – the only thing that mattered was the mile and the moment we were in. My world was in the van, while my wife was just a phone call away on the shiny new phone I had presented her with before we departed. Life was good.

'Buckle up, boys,' I said, beaming to myself now. 'Let's make some memories.'

*   *   *

Across Scotland, there's no shortage of nice, quiet places to pitch up for the night. It's such a stunning country, where wild camping is permitted and offers wide open spaces that can transport you from all the worries in the world. I had an airbed in the back of the van, which fitted in alongside three dog beds. I also packed a hammock, which quickly became my favourite thing. I'd park up near trees off some remote country lane, tie one end to a trunk and the other to the roofbar, and then just lie there with my dogs lolling in the sun on the grass. It was blissful. Max, Paddy and Harry were quite content, while I was free to read a book without a worry in the world. At sundown, following a nice long walk to explore our new surroundings, we'd tuck up together in the back of the van. Naturally, no spaniel can ever lie still for more than a few minutes, even when they're exhausted. It meant I'd wake up momentarily and then nod off again, thinking what a lucky man I was. Nobody bothered us, we could just be.

By the time we departed Inverness and set out on the NC500 it felt like we had become kings of the road. The weather largely stayed on our side all week, while the landscape continued to open up on a breathtaking scale. We'd follow roads through the heart of great glens, the tarmac like a ribbon amid heather and streams, and the dogs savoured every moment. Harry even began to venture forward to join us on the middle seat. There, Max would lean against him. It was the way he had always sat, but as time passed so it became more pronounced. Harry took it in his stride and locked his gaze on the road ahead. I sometimes wondered what was on his mind. It seemed to me that he was looking so far into the distance that he could see things long before me. Just as Max called upon his support from the passenger seat, I found comfort in that from behind the wheel.

As for Paddy, stationed at the rear window where he always liked to be, I knew exactly what he was looking out for.

'Over there! Do you see it?'

The first time I spotted a red deer, as we barrelled along an A road with not a soul in sight, all three dogs sat up to attention and looked to where I was pointing. There it was, bounding away across the heather at the sound of our approach. The creature's russet coat was striking, but it was the antlers that caused me to slow the van to a halt so we could watch it.

'Wow!' I said, having grabbed a few photos on my phone before it finally disappeared behind boulders. 'What a rarity! We're so lucky to have seen something like that. What a picture that will be!'

At that point, I don't think I had come to appreciate how Highland wildlife wakes up towards the end of each day. As soon as the sun dropped behind the mountains and the evening settled in, it seemed like every red deer in the region came out to play. Quite literally, hundreds of them came out as if to demonstrate that in fact it was a human being and three dogs that were in the minority. We were still driving at the time, but every minute or less we'd have to slow right down and go wide.

'It's like they own the road,' I muttered as the dogs revolved around the van to keep them in eyeshot as we passed by. 'Maybe they do,' I reflected further and decided that perhaps we should pull in soon and pitch up.

*   *   *

We had been driving parallel with a river, which seemed like a lovely place to stop. Parking at the water's edge, the dogs jumped out and of course jumped straight in. After a long day of driving, I followed suit and we had a great splash around in the last light. That evening, the dogs ate from their bowls under the stars while I used my portable gas cooker to make supper. It was perfect, but eventually the midges encouraged us to bed.

'Good night,' I said to my three favourite boys. 'Mind the bed bugs don't bite and when I say "bed bugs", you know I mean midges and mosquitoes.'

Before switching off my head torch, I made sure the van was free from midges. Even so, I couldn't be certain. In fact, I lay awake that night convinced I could hear a faint buzzing sound. Eventually, I reminded myself that midges were harmless – their bites could be an irritation, but we weren't going to die out here.

A short while later, just as I was drifting into sleep, the entire van jolted.

'What the …?'

It wasn't just me who sat bolt upright, though only Max, Paddy and Harry started growling when we found ourselves rocked once again. In a blink, there in the dark I stopped feeling under threat from tiny insects and worried that an axe murderer was paying us a visit. I glanced at Paddy, who was leading the vocal response.

'Growl louder,' I whispered. 'Unleash your inner guard dog!'

The third time that the vehicle rocked on its suspension and continued for a good minute, I felt I was in a living horror movie. By now, the dogs were openly barking. I needed them to sound furious and not like three high-pitched Scooby-Doos, which they did when spooked. Still wearing my headtorch, I switched it on and pointed the beam over the front seats and through the windows. I expected to see a bunch of youths take flight. Instead, the light just reflected against the glass and dazzled me. It also did nothing to deter the ongoing assault from outside.

It left me with no option too. I had to take responsibility for the situation. With the van squeaking on its springs once more, I grasped Paddy by his collar, just in case it was kids out to scare us and they needed to see the one dog that at least looked like he could bare his teeth, and hauled open the door. In response, a hoard of red deer peered back at us. Those closest to the van stopped rubbing their flanks against it, which is when I realised what was going on, while Max, Paddy and Harry shared their look of utter surprise.

Momentarily.

The din when they kicked off, combined with the sudden scattering of an antlered herd that had found a good scratching post, was explosive. I held onto the dogs for as long as I could, before all three scrambled after them as they took to the glen. Just to be sure they arrived there safely. I knew the deer would come to no harm. My spaniels love a little chase, but soon peeled away and returned, panting hard. And when they did hop back into the van a minute later, having clearly been outrun, I settled down with them, reassured by their presence. Even if Max, Paddy and Harry lacked ferocity, their loyalty was enough. We were a long way from home, after all, and in the middle of nowhere, but with dogs you're never alone.

Following that encounter, as we continued with our journey to the West Coast, Paddy kept close watch for his newfound nemesis. At night he got to grips with his growling so at least it sounded like he was serious and that meant we were left in peace. On the road, he would prick up his ears at the sight of a pair of antlers in the bracken. I felt no need to stop and take a photograph – we had seen enough red deer for one lifetime.

5
Dog Years

HAVING SET OUT ON A 500-mile road trip, we ended up covering almost three times that distance. I wasn't concerned about how far we'd travelled. With Angela's blessing, our seven-day tour extended into a two-week adventure. I just loved to drive with my dogs. We didn't have to be anywhere for our tea at five o'clock or anything like that. First thing each morning, I would settle behind the wheel of the van, look across at Max and say, 'Right, where would you like to go?' And together, we had the time of our lives.

Eventually, we made it around to Scotland's West Coast. In my view, it boasts some of the best beaches in the world. We would walk across those white sands, with not a soul in sight, and enjoy that time to ourselves. While Paddy and Harry switched back and forth across the dunes, investigating every tuffet of grass, dear Max would happily toddle along beside me. Often the two of us would sit looking out to sea as the other two gamboled in the shallows.

Just as we were enjoying the tail end of our grand tour around Scotland, however, Max got sick.

I've always been sensitive to his health and welfare. Max had been through a tough life before we met and I wanted him to make up for that lost time. It came as a shock to see him take such a downturn, in which he became listless and clearly in discomfort. One minute he was my old Max and the next he had lost that spark and any sense of appetite. What food he ate, he couldn't keep down and I panicked.

By dawn the next day, following an overnight drive, we arrived in the town of Fort William. We have good friends there and they kindly arranged for me to bring Max to their vet.

'We've had a scare,' I told Angela when I called her afterwards, 'but he's going to be OK.'

As soon as the vet began to examine Max, I felt relieved that he was in good hands. On my own, I just felt so alarmed and helpless. Calm and reassuring, she prescribed Max some medication to settle his stomach. Having found no further cause for concern, she suggested that he rest for a few days. I felt that another peaceful trip to the beach would be the best medicine for him, so we took the ferry to the Isle of Mull and stayed in one place. We kept things nice and simple for him, from sitting outside the van, enjoying the fresh air, to stretching our legs with a visit to the water's edge. Max picked up considerably, which came as a huge relief. A few days into his recuperation, as I started to think it must have been something he'd eaten, he took a turn for the worse. The vomiting and listlessness returned and I knew that I couldn't simply hope it would pass.

This time, we packed our bags and headed straight home. On the way, I called our local vet. I hated to see Max suffering – I wanted to make him better, but felt so helpless. It was a very long drive back to the Lake District, which was enough for me to stew and start fearing the worst. Max was in his senior years after all and with twelve years of age came vulnerabilities, so it served as both a surprise and a relief when the vet gave him an injection to settle things and assured me he'd be fine. He was just under the weather, with no further course of action required than rest. As we left the surgery, however, he put something into words that I found hard to handle.

'Max is getting on in life,' he said. 'Just keep that in mind.'

When we finally walked through the front door, Max had recovered sufficiently to light up with Paddy and Harry on seeing Angela.

'You probably think I overreacted,' I said when he broke off from circling her, his tail wagging like a wind-up toy, in order to take himself off to his basket.

'Oh, Kerry,' she said. 'Everyone knows how much Max means to you.'

I couldn't even hear her say this without my eyes filling with tears. It was something I never liked to think about. Only now, for Max's sake as much as mine, it felt like the subject was something I had to address.

*   *   *

You think a dog will be with you forever, but then life seems to move a little faster for them. They say there are seven human years squeezed into one canine year, after all. I liked to think that's why dogs made the most of every day. Also, I now realised it meant time would run out on him before I was ready.

I wanted to grow old with Max, only now he had grown old before me.

Despite this turn of events that brought us home early, nothing could overshadow the fact that we'd had a road trip to remember. I'd enjoyed every moment and so too had all three dogs. We had made those memories and in some ways that helped me come to terms with the future ahead. I saw Max in a new light now. He was still here, curled up in his basket as he liked to do, but now I registered a depth to his sleep. He was tired, as we all become as life slows down. I had always taken great care to exercise him within his means, but now that boundless world he once enjoyed was shrinking. He still loved to go out on the fells with Paddy and Harry, who always went that little bit further – I just needed to make sure that we continued to tailor everything so that Max was at the heart of it all.

Five years earlier, Max was unlucky enough to get in the way of a clumsy Labrador. One minute my dog was just trotting along, the next the Lab had come careering across the grass and accidentally knocked him off his feet. The result had been a broken shoulder for poor Max. He'd bounced back from it like a true spaniel, but over time that joint caused him problems. It would take him a while to get going and as the years progressed, it set in as a permanent feature. He'd been keeping by my side for some time, long before our visit to Scotland. To accommodate for his dodgy shoulder, he'd even developed a slight limp. Our vet kept a close eye on it and assured me that while Max loved to walk, the exercise could only help with his flexibility.

Naturally, I made sure that we kept within his limits. Max himself knew when it was time to stop and rest, and we had built that into our routine. As we also shared clips of our walks online, it was only natural that sometimes people would point his limp out to me – they always meant well and I appreciated the concern. After Scotland, however, I found such comments reminded me of something I'd only just come to terms with myself. I still found it hard to accept that one day he wouldn't be by my side. I even resolved to *be more spaniel* – as I often joked – by making every day count. Even so, it pained me to think that people thought I was unaware that he was an elderly dog with frailties. It made me question whether the kindest thing I could do was to let Max retire from public life.

I dwelled on the matter for some time and talked things through at length with Angela. Over the years, Max had raised thousands of pounds for charity and transformed lives on so many levels. He brought happiness to people. To those who struggled, he gave them hope. My priority was always Max's welfare and when I framed it like this, I realised that withdrawing him from the wider world would make no difference to his quality of life. We would still head for the hills at every opportunity, even if our walks were shorter than they might once have been. As for the fundraising events, Max loved to be with people. If I called a halt to those ventures, I would simply be denying him an experience he really enjoyed. Yes, it would take away some of the pressure I put myself under to meet the demand for calendars and group walks, but that paled into insignificance when I thought about the impact Max had on the wider world. All I had to do was remind myself of the qualities he showed me when I was at my lowest. With compassion and commitment, combined with a sensitivity to his needs, I could help Max enjoy the rest of his life and continue to make a difference to lives around the world.

So, rather than pull away from Max's Facebook community, I decided that in fact we could put more into it without asking any more from him. Every year, the demand for calendars had grown. I have always loved photographing the dogs on the fells and enjoy making a selection that tells a story over twelve months. It was just the scale of each annual production that I found so challenging and this came down to space. It had reached a point where I'd pick up all the boxes from the printer's and then find myself at a loss as to what to do with them on stacking them inside the hall. As I also brought my locksmith tools indoors at night, it really was beginning to feel more like a storage unit than our house. I also needed to consider my back, which was the cause of all my problems after the road accident. Quite simply, I didn't want to keep lugging stuff from one room to another just so that Angela and I could live our lives.

With Max uppermost on my mind, keen to find a way to spend more time with him while supporting his online community, I realised there was only one solution: it was time we found a place during each working day that we could call our own.

What we needed, as I told Angela on pitching my proposal, was a Paw Store.

'Well,' she said, and I could literally see her looking forward to reclaiming the house as our home, 'I think that's an excellent idea!'

As a project, the search for suitable premises really helped me to overcome the realisation that Max was in his senior years. He still served as my head of security for the locksmith business. As that just amounted to sitting in the passenger seat to keep me company, with

Paddy and Harry in the back, I didn't feel like it was too much for him. I wanted to establish a base for us during the day that was comfortable for us all, provided space for storage and allowed me to create a divide between work and home.

So, when I heard about the availability of a small business unit on a farm just outside Keswick, we jumped at the chance to check it out. As soon as I turned off the road and followed a steep track through the farm gates, I had a feeling it would work out just fine. We hadn't even seen inside, but when I glanced in my rear-view mirror and saw Paddy gazing out of the back, I knew we'd found the right place.

'Look at that, boys,' I said, pulling up for a moment so that I could turn and see for myself.

Behind us, beyond the River Greta that ran like a seam between rolling woodland, the mighty fells of Lonscale and Latrigg reached across the skyline. We had walked every hilltop and mountain surrounding us, but those magnificent landmarks had always been a favourite. We'd enjoyed so many happy walks over there and to think it could be so close meant my mind was made up before we'd even toured the unit.

*   *   *

Within the course of a few days, Max, Paddy, Harry and I worked hard to make that place feel like a home from home. We transported all the boxes and my locksmith gear across and installed a sofa and two comfortable chairs. I even remembered food and water bowls for the dogs. As I put up shelves and set up my computer on a desk, my four-legged colleagues invested their energies in testing the furniture for comfort.

'So, do we approve?' I asked them as they snored soundly.

I put in a kettle and a microwave and popped a wooden bench outside so that we could enjoy some fresh air over a brew. It suited us perfectly, I decided, on packing up calendars for postage one morning soon after we'd moved in. The change of scene worked wonders for my motivation, while Max, Paddy and Harry were so in tune with their new surroundings it seemed as if they'd been there for a lifetime. Over the following weeks, I really came to appreciate the divide between my work and home. I put in long hours at The Paw Store, as we called it, either focusing on calendars, community and charity projects, or as a base for my locksmith business. For years, the community had been asking me for Max memorabilia, such as woolly hats and scarves, or mugs or photographic prints. It had always struck me as a lovely idea. Working from my little study in the house, however, I just didn't feel I had the space or the energy to create quality, meaningful products.

Now we had The Paw Store and a renewed appreciation of the joy Max brought to people, I set out to meet that demand. Dealing with manufacturers online took me back to my former career in agricultural sales before the road accident forced me to stop work. It meant that I was on familiar territory but without the daily grind of a long commute or the stress of targets to meet and bosses to please. Now it was just me and my dogs, tucked away in our own little world in the Lake District, and I adored it.

With a farm track just yards away, and paths in every direction, we could take off for walks at any time throughout each day. It became a starting point for little explorations, with Max at my side and Paddy leading Harry. Then, with our work complete, we'd jump in the van and go home to spend time with Angela.

This new way of living suited us all. Angela would join us for walks around the lake if the weather was nice and we regularly took the dogs up to The Lingholm Kitchen & Walled Garden for a bite to eat. Ever since he came into our lives, Max had been a regular visitor. Even if he didn't bound inside with the same energy he once possessed, it would always be a place where he felt safe. It helped that he was often recognised, along with Paddy and Harry, and so could expect lots of cuddles and attention. Dogs have a knack of bringing everyone together and serving as a topic for conversation.

We've met lots of lovely people this way. On one occasion in the autumn of that year, in fact, a chance encounter would go on to transform our lives forever.

6

Continuation

THE PAW STORE WAS KEEPING ME BUSY. While my four-legged work colleagues napped on the sofa – knowing they'd never get fired – each day I'd spend the time fulfilling orders for Max memorabilia, dealing with media enquiries or invitations to give talks, as well as hatching plans for charity walks. Even when I was run off my feet, however, it still felt like shared time with Max, Paddy and Harry. Every now and then I'd put the phone on silent, prepare a brew and take it outside so we could sit on the bench together and remind ourselves that time was precious.

It was during those short breaks, in which Max often dozed across my lap as the other two sniffed around the farm track, that I found myself returning to the thought that he wouldn't be here forever. I had come to terms with what was a basic fact of life for us all but it was always there, surfacing in my mind whenever I had time on my hands. Rather than brood about it, I had learned that the best antidote was to spend quality moments with Max, Paddy, Harry and Angela. As a result, after a lovely walk one weekend, we had dropped into The Lingholm for a spot of lunch. The dogs always stationed themselves under the long benches in the dining area. It was nice and quiet for them down there, plus they were in prime position for any food that happened to drop off our forks. They weren't exactly out of sight, however, and inevitably three swishing tails between the chairs always drew attention.

That day, as we settled in, I noticed another diner smiling at the sight of three dogs under our feet. She was alone at the next table and I acknowledged her with a cheery nod.

'If only my Springer sat that quietly,' she joked, which earned my full attention.

I always loved to meet other spaniel owners. All dogs are magic, but there's just something about the positive energy this breed can bring that unites people. Within minutes, she had joined us at our table to meet Max, Paddy and Harry, and there Angela and I learned that this was a moment of light for her in a week of disappointment and frustration.

Amanda lived in Jersey with her family and a Springer Spaniel called Archie. She and her husband had flown over from their Channel Islands home, where she ran a veterinary practice, to take part in a Lake District triathlon. Amanda, sounding cross, explained to us that on arrival, she had learned that the event had been cancelled at short notice.

'Apparently there is an algae in the lake which means we can't swim,' she told us, 'so they called the whole thing off.'

'The water has been like that for most of the summer,' I said, which apparently cut to the heart of her annoyance.

'And I could've saved myself a wasted journey!' she added.

Just then, perhaps sensing that she was having a hard time, Harry popped up from under the table to rest his head on Amanda's knee. She looked down, placed a hand on his head and breathed out in a release of tension.

'I'm not usually like this,' she grinned and admitted that Rob – who was back at their lodgings – would've been mortified. 'Maybe I just miss my dog.'

'Well, think of Harry as a stand-in for Archie,' I said. 'He's at your service for as long as you need him.'

From that moment on, having got it out of her system, Amanda relaxed considerably. She even laughed about the situation and admitted there could be worse places to spend a few days until her flight home. Angela and I really enjoyed her company and we soon found ourselves back on the subject closest to our hearts. It was interesting to hear from a Springer Spaniel owner who was also qualified in caring for animal welfare. Amanda understood dogs and it was heartening to hear her compliment us on taking such good care of our three boys.

'My Archie is only a few years behind Max,' she said at one point. 'Having Harry and Paddy for company must keep him young at heart.'

'Would you consider another one?' asked Angela. 'A companion for Archie?'

Amanda looked at me, as if hoping I might share my experience.

'Max saved my life,' I said candidly. 'Paddy and Harry remind me to make the most of every day. Spaniels are just such joyful creatures that I could never be without them.'

With her hand pressed to Harry's coat, Amanda reflected on this for a moment. Then she seemed to come back to us and consulted her watch.

'Rob will be wondering where I am,' she said before playfully scratching Harry behind his ears, 'but thank you for cheering me up. I really needed that.'

'Well, we'll be here at the same time tomorrow,' said Angela. 'As will the dogs.'

*   *   *

It had been one of those chance encounters where we all just clicked. Amanda and my wife had a great deal in common that went beyond dealing with muddy pawprints in the hallway, while I found it strangely comforting to meet someone who was also navigating life with an elderly Springer Spaniel who meant so much to them. At that time, my focus was on continuing to provide Max with the best possible life. Even though he was winding down, he still possessed the same uplifting spirit I had first encountered all those years ago. At the same time, if I were to lose him I couldn't imagine how I would cope without Harry and Paddy at my side. That evening, as the dogs dozed in front of the woodburner, I dwelled on the subject with Angela.

'Paddy and Harry learned a great deal from Max,' she said. 'As puppies, they looked up to him. Now I see his qualities in them. Both dogs are just as biddable, calm and gentle, and they look out for each other.'

'That's Max,' I agreed, feeling comforted by the way she saw things.

'They bring continuation,' said Angela. 'He'll live on in them after he's gone.'

*   *   *

No one likes to think about a time when a beloved pet is no longer there. It's a painful downside of animal companionship. As much as it hurt me just to think about it, I had learned that coming to terms with canine mortality was an important part of the process. Having rushed home from Scotland, shocked into confronting Max's age and fragility, I had gone on to make changes to my working life so our time together didn't feel so squeezed. Having Paddy and Harry in the mix softened the edges of what was basically an inevitability. One day Max would not be with us, yet I knew his spirit would be present in the two dogs who followed in his pawprints.

Just as humans from different generations can often bring out the best in each other, it seemed to me that a puppy could be a fitting companion for Amanda's old dog. It was a chance to pass on a legacy, I thought to myself, on turning in that night and waking the next morning for our early walk. It stayed on my mind because it had struck a chord, I think. Without doubt, Max had made an impact on people. He had helped so many and now I realised that in time it would fall to Paddy and Harry to carry his legacy onwards. That need for continuation, which summed up what I was thinking, seemed to be shared by Amanda in her relationship with their Springer, Archie. So, when Angela and I returned to The Lingholm for lunch, it felt like the appearance of a kindred spirit when she appeared along with her husband, Rob.

'Amanda insisted that I meet you both,' he said as we shook hands. 'And your wonderful dogs.'

It was a warm afternoon in late September and so we had chosen to sit outside. We had quite clearly run into spaniel people because Rob and Amanda were so natural with Max, Paddy and Harry. Within minutes, the dogs had made friends for life.

'You must be missing Archie,' said Angela.

'Always.' Rob had seemed especially struck by Harry and Paddy. I noticed Amanda reading his expression, as if to see how he'd respond to the two younger dogs.

'Max was great when they were very young,' I said, which was mischievous of me but I could tell he was on board. 'Paddy hung off his ear a little too much for his liking, but now they're inseparable for different reasons.'

Amanda smiled as if she knew full well what I was pitching here.

'Well, that's good to know,' she said, 'because we're thinking about a puppy.'

'How lovely,' said Angela.

'Do you know what?' I said and shared something I'd been secretly considering since our early-morning walk. 'I think Paddy would make a great dad.'

Now my wife looked at me in complete surprise, while Amanda and Rob seemed to converse without words as married couples often can.

'If you're serious,' said Amanda after a moment, 'then we couldn't think of a better father.'

'But who would we breed him with?' asked Angela.

As if in response, a couple climbed the steps from the car park. They were heading for the entrance to the kitchen, but what commanded our attention was the female Springer Spaniel that led the way. We must have been staring as if destiny had just come calling because the couple looked at us quizzically.

'Well, she's nice!' I declared, a little louder than intended and then realised I would have to explain myself.

The Springer who had just bounded into our lives was called Bella. A beautiful and lively dog, she wore an expression of pure sunshine. As it turned out, I had met her owners once before. Lisa and Adam are absolute gold, they really are the nicest couple. In fact, I'd had the pleasure of running into them when Paddy was just six months old. We'd been up the hills along with Max, where I was taking photographs of them for the Facebook community page. Lisa and Adam are keen runners. They were out with Bella, who is a year or so older than Paddy, and had stopped to say hello – it's almost a legal requirement among spaniel owners and a lovely way to meet new people.

Having drawn attention to myself in a weird way, I breathed a sigh of relief when the couple appeared to recognise me. Then Max, Paddy and Harry emerged from under the table to say hello to Bella and suddenly it felt like a gathering in the making. I introduced Amanda and Rob, explaining to Lisa and Adam how we had met. As all four spaniels were so happy to be in each other's company, we invited them to join us at our table.

'We were just saying that Paddy would make a great dad and then you came along with his dream date.'

I was half-joking as I said this, but Lisa and Adam didn't laugh. Instead, they exchanged glances and told me that they'd often thought about breeding Bella. It had simply been a question of finding the right dog.

'Why don't we swap numbers?' suggested Adam after what turned out to be a lovely half an hour of great company and good coffee. 'We should all have a think and take it from there.'

*   *   *

Back home, Angela believed that she could read my mind.

'Why don't you just admit you want another puppy?' she said, laughing at the same time.

'I don't!' I said. 'Hand on heart, now isn't the right time. Max is my priority and I'm very happy with the Brown-Legged Gang as it is.'

'So, why are you so keen to breed Paddy?'

I told her about my thoughts on continuation. At a time when a sense of sadness crept around the edges of my relationship with Max, this was a way to bring a sense of joy and renewal into the equation. Paddy is such an amazing character. He just rolls through life with confidence and compassion and I felt it would be so lovely to see those qualities shine in another generation.

'He can be a hands-on father,' I said, 'and Max will be spared all the ear-chewing.'

It was a light-hearted exchange, but I knew that Angela understood my reasons. Now was not the time for a puppy in our household, but it lifted my spirits to think Paddy would be helping others in his own special way. I just had to remind myself that it might all lead to nothing. The whole proposal had come together by chance and I knew there was every possibility that Adam and Lisa would reconsider so I put it to the back of my mind. At best, I thought perhaps they might get in touch within a few weeks to let me know one way or the other. The last thing I expected was for my phone to ring that same evening.

'We've given it some thought,' said Adam, 'Bella is just coming into season and we'd like to go ahead.'

Now, there is something very awkward about arranging to breed dogs. Adam and I are both sensible adults and yet as we attempted to hatch a plan we both stumbled and sniggered our way through the details. Eventually, we settled on a simple arrangement in which he and I would bring Paddy and Bella to a quiet woodland car park near Keswick to do the deed. Naturally, when I pulled up with Paddy to find Adam and Bella waiting for us, it all felt very furtive.

'Shall we do it here?' asked Adam, looking around.

A couple of cars were parked nearby, but we were the only people around. Even so, it didn't feel quite right.

'Let's head up the track,' I suggested as Paddy sniffed around Bella, 'and hope we can get this done quickly.'

We only had to walk for a couple of minutes, following the path between late autumnal trees until we found a suitable spot. I looked around. We were out of eyeshot from the car park. Also, we weren't doing anything wrong, I had to remind myself. At the same time, and clearly picking up on signals that Adam and I couldn't detect, Paddy circled around Bella and attempted to mount her.

'She's quite a small dog,' I observed as Paddy tried to wrap his great front legs around her.

'Yeah, I'm not sure we thought this bit through,' said Adam, grimacing as Bella ducked from underneath him.

'Come on, old son,' I said under my breath. 'You can do it.'

When Paddy made a second attempt, we both cheered quietly to ourselves. We were so focused on the action, in fact, that neither Adam nor I noticed the three elderly ramblers who came down the track towards us at that moment. It was only when one of them pointedly cleared their throat as we were basically blocking their path that we both gasped, jumped apart and pretended we hadn't noticed the two dogs attempting to perform right in front of us.

'Good afternoon,' I said weakly and Adam followed suit.

The three hikers passed by, looking at us like we should be locked up, which only left us both to dissolve into fits of laugher once they'd gone.

As for Paddy and Bella, it was clear that our canine couple were struggling to connect on account of their difference in size. Every time Paddy jumped on, Bella would just walk away.

'We should get going,' I suggested finally, 'before we're arrested.'

Adam laughed again as we called the dogs to follow us back to the car park.

'Maybe next time we should find somewhere more private,' he said. 'And dignified for the dogs.'

*　　*　　*

That evening, as I shared my story of events with Angela, I waited for her to stop cringing and suggested that perhaps it wasn't to be. Bella would only be in season for a short while longer before that window of opportunity closed for the foreseeable future.

'I don't want Paddy to get stressed about it,' I said. 'You know? With the weight of expectation.'

Back with Harry and Max, Paddy was snoring in his basket like the job was as good as done. When I looked back at Angela, I found she was already considering me.

'What's the rush?' she asked. 'Paddy and Bella have only just met. Perhaps they should relax and get to know each other.'

I chuckled at the suggestion.

'You make it sound like a romance,' I said.

Angela didn't reply straight away.

'It'll be at least six months before Bella comes into season again,' she pointed out. 'That's plenty of opportunity for love to blossom.'

I looked at Paddy and laughed, unaware that a global event was set to restrict our lives beyond all imagination. In the world of isolation that we were all about to enter, a pandemic lasting seemingly without end, I would be reminded never to take companionship for granted.

Part Two

7

Making Time for the Things We Love

TOWARDS THE VERY END OF 2019, it came as a relief when the demand for calendars dropped away. I have always found that everyone wants them in time for Christmas and so I did everything I could to make sure they arrived ready to be wrapped. This meant I spent weeks packing and posting, but I loved just being with the dogs in The Paw Store. As a result, it didn't feel like work. Having that space together was so inspiring and I found myself getting creative.

'Are we ready?' I asked the boys as they posed for me on the sofa, sporting baseball caps with Max's name and pawprint embroidered on the front. None of them could see out, but they sat happily while I got the shot we needed. 'Perfect. Thank you! You make great models.'

With the calendars hanging in people's homes around the world, I had turned my attention to building an online shop. It had started as a response to requests from Max's Facebook community. As people wanted to identify with him in any way they could, my early offerings of hats, scarves and T-shirts expanded to gifts and homewares. Max had obliged me with a pawprint, which became his motif, while it was orange-coloured products that proved to be the most popular because they matched the harness that he wore.

Every morning after our early walk, we'd head up to the store for breakfast. Max, Paddy and Harry had quickly adapted to eating at the workplace. For one thing, they could scatter kibble from their bowls as they ate without me having to worry about Angela. She didn't like mess, even though Max was always on hand to clean up after the other two. Then, over coffee, I'd update the online shop, process orders that had come in overnight or check in on the production of new items. If we needed to visit the Post Office, all three dogs would come with me. Not only did they love any excuse for a journey, but they also enjoyed the attention they would always receive as I waited in line at the counter.

Increasingly, I tried to fit all my locksmith work into the afternoons. My head of security and his two apprentices were quite happy to accompany me, so before we set off I made sure that we had all eaten well and enjoyed a good walk. Towards supper, we'd head home to see Angela. With no more boxes or tools for her to trip over, it seemed as if the arrangement worked just as well for her. As we moved into the New Year, she even encouraged Max to sit beside her.

'You've just made his day,' I said, the first time he crept up into the space between the front seats and leaned against her.

'Well, it can only get better for him,' she said, laughing, as she put a protective arm around him. 'My dad is joining us for supper later.'

*   *   *

Alistair was in his late eighties and lived with a heart condition. I was really fond of him. He was a lovely, cheery man who had welcomed me into his family all those years ago at a time when I'd never known what it was like to feel supported by one. Born and bred in Keswick, he had lost his wife, Angela's mother, several years earlier and moved into sheltered accommodation near us. Like so many widowers, he was as proud as he was lonely. Our house was always open to him and it wasn't only Angela and I who were always pleased to see him. Max had a special relationship with Alistair and not just because my father-in-law would load up his pockets with dog biscuits before visiting. I suppose they were both two wise but frail old guys who understood each other. Either way, it was always so nice to see Max greet him every time he visited, followed closely by Harry and Paddy, who never knowingly missed out on a treat.

In the same way, Alistair always looked forward to our charity walks. He'd hung up his hiking boots some time ago, but always came out to see everyone off and welcome them back. Then he'd take to his chair with a cup of tea and a slice of cake and chat away for hours. People adored my father-in-law, as did all the dogs, and I looked forward to telling him all about the events I had planned for the year. For one thing, it would be Max's thirteenth birthday that August. It was quite an age in dog years and I wanted to be sure that we made it an event to remember.

That evening, with Max at his feet, Alistair asked with interest about his recent adventures. We chatted about the school visits and the workplace talks and he would peer down at Max and remark on what a clever boy he'd been. Alistair seemed to embody the spirit of so many people who belonged to our Facebook community. He was such a sociable and outgoing guy but circumstance meant those connections weren't always easily available. It was Max who brought out the best in him – it was always such a pleasure to see them together.

For a season that was often cold, blustery and wet in the Lake District, I felt so positive in those first few months of 2020. My work as a locksmith was still demanding, but I loved our little Paw Store and made time for the dogs, my family and new friends. Paddy and Bella might not have done the deed when she was last in season, yet it led to a blossoming friendship. Adam and Lisa would bring her out on walks with us, not just so the dogs could get to know each other but because we all got on so well. We'd aim to meet up once or twice a week, whatever the weather, and it was so lovely to see Paddy and Bella bonding throughout that time. As spring beckoned that year, Bella had become an honorary member of the Brown-Legged Gang. They had a shared passion for tennis balls and when Paddy once dropped his so that his new friend could pick it up, we read between the lines. We'd joke about their growing love affair, but sometimes the way they looked at each other made me think there really had to be a spark.

We still had plans for puppies and this way it seemed more meaningful. Our friends in Jersey, Amanda and Rob, shared our outlook. With tongue in cheek, they felt sure that come the summer when Bella was next in season, she would only have eyes for one spaniel.

Life was good. I had a renewed appreciation of time with Max and whenever Bella joined us, it reminded me that in time a new generation would bring that sense of continuation. Unusually, by early March we had already put the wet weather behind us. With dry ground and clement days, I'd take the dogs back up to the fells. With Max in mind, we didn't go far. Often I'd drive to a quiet spot, where Paddy and Harry could run around and leave my old spaniel and me to admire breathtaking views. Surrounded by mountains, it was easy to forget that a wider world existed beyond the horizon.

Back home, whenever I put on the news, it began to feel like an unwelcome reality was pressing in on us.

For at that time, a global sense of uncertainty and concern had begun to gather strength in response to a new and infectious virus. It had already affected some countries quite severely and now cases were occurring in the UK.

'Do you think it'll reach us?' asked Angela as we listened to the headlines one morning. With every day that passed, worrying stories about the coronavirus had begun to close in on us all. The UK government were talking about putting measures in place that would pause our everyday lives. Angela sounded rightfully concerned and so I was thankful that the boys were with us when she asked me.

'Whatever happens,' I said, 'these guys will help us to stay positive.'

In that moment, neither of us could have imagined that within the space of a week our world would stop turning. It was the same for everyone across the UK as restrictions came into effect. Suddenly, everything changed. It was a shock for Angela, who had to put her hairdressing business on hold. The only time I saw her smile in those early days was when I discovered that I provided an essential service: as a locksmith, I was a *key* worker in every sense.

'Oh, Kerry,' she said with a chuckle.

'It was funny the first time a customer cracked that joke,' I told her, before giving in to a grin. 'I guess I'm just going to have to get used to it.'

Angela's smile faded. Concern returned to her expression. We were standing in the back garden at the time, enjoying some fresh air.

'Everything just seems so different,' she said.

'Well, there's one thing that hasn't changed ...' I invited her to consider Max, Harry and Paddy, who were sniffing around the flower beds and stretching their legs. 'The great thing about dogs is that they've no idea what's going on in the news, but they do know when things are troubling you.'

Angela considered this for a moment then she crouched down and called them. All three trotted across as if to remind her that she still mattered.

'We're here for each other,' I said. 'We'll be OK.'

*　　*　　*

During lockdown, the number of vacant properties I was commissioned to watch over as a locksmith climbed considerably. From stately homes to holiday cabins, so many places were lying empty and often the owners lived far away. Sometimes they would ask me to check that windows and doors were secure and provide a presence to deter uninvited guests. On other occasions, I would receive a call as key holder because an alarm had been tripped. Serving as my security team, Max, Paddy and Harry saw off any squirrels that had somehow found their way indoors. More often than not, they just liked to poke about places in search of dropped snacks.

Tiptoeing around some of the bigger places behind them, I was thankful for their company. There was one address in particular, however, where it wasn't creepy at all. In fact, it actually felt like a privilege and a pleasure to sweep the property and surrounding grounds.

Surrounded by landscaped gardens and woodland that led up to the fells, this National Trust property near Grasmere was normally open to the public and bustling with visitors. It felt so strange to find ourselves quite alone up there, but also strikingly peaceful. I had been asked to check the place over on a regular basis and so it became somewhere for us to walk. I had a letter author-ising me to be there for work purposes. We never saw a soul. For Paddy, I hoped it made up for the fact that Bella had suddenly vanished. He didn't understand about the measures we'd had to take to minimise the spread of the virus. Through his spaniel eyes, his special friend had simply disappeared from his life.

'We'll see her again,' I promised him as we sat on the ridge above the woodland one lunchtime. 'If there's one thing we can say about all dogs, they're loyal.'

It was a troubling time for everyone. I recognised why we needed to stay at home and learn about social distancing but having locked myself away once before, during that troubling time after the road accident when depression ruled my life, I worried about the impact it could have upon the mental health of the population. Above all, on account of his age and frailty, I was concerned about Alistair. Every time I answered a call-out to replace or repair a lock, I had visions of coming into contact with the virus and somehow passing it from Angela to her father. Even though she had to keep her distance from him, it still bothered me.

As lockdown stretched on, I found that customers began cancelling non-emergency appointments for fittings and repairs. While it disrupted my diary, weirdly I felt only relief. I still enjoyed checking in on the vacant properties along with my dogs, it's just the risks I associated with the other side of my work became too great. And so, after more than a decade of work as a locksmith, I decided to wind down the business.

*   *   *

It came to me one day at The Paw Store. Before lockdown, I had idly considered hiring a part-time assistant to help me with the volume of online orders. As much as I loved putting Max at the centre of this new line of work, it took up so much time. Then, with restrictions in place, I was thankful for staying as a one-man, three-dog operation. It meant I was within restrictions to continue working at the store. Not only did it get us out of the house, but it also meant that I was on hand to deal with a huge upswing in demand.

'People have time on their hands,' I said to the boys as they watched me from the sofa. Just weeks into lockdown, I found myself fighting to keep up with orders.

First, I had responded to requests to expand the range of Max-related products available, from coasters to cuddly toys, and worked hard to put quality at the forefront of design and production. Then, once the postwoman dropped off boxes of products from the wholesale factories I commissioned to create my stock, I'd spend all morning fulfilling orders.

I was responsible for everything, working off the beaten track with my three best friends for company, and I couldn't have been happier. By comparison, when switching to my role as a locksmith in the afternoons, I felt tense working around people and worried about a virus that we knew so little about. I was at my most content alone with my dogs. One morning, as I hurried to get everything packaged up in time for the Post Office, now opening on a limited basis, I looked at Max and asked him a question only I could answer: 'Does it have to be like this?'

I set down the package I'd been wrapping and joined him on the sofa. All of a sudden, time seemed to pause for me. In the silence, as Paddy and Harry hopped up beside us, I realised for the second time in my life I had allowed myself to get boxed in. The first time, following my road accident, it was physical and mental pain that left me feeling like a prisoner inside my own home. I didn't venture outside for months on end and simply sat behind closed curtains, feeling helpless. Meeting Max had helped me find the strength to make a positive change: he had shown me that with support, we can all find ways to live our lives to the full.

Now I knew we had another opportunity to break free. This time, I wasn't trapped inside a house but caught between two career paths. The Paw Store was a new venture, but it allowed me to devote my working life to my dogs. It brought out the best in me, while my afternoons as a locksmith had increasingly felt like a chore. Yes, it had a reliable income attached to it, but that wasn't as important to me as my happiness. I still enjoyed some aspects of the work and looked forward to sweeping the majestic grounds of that National Trust property, but nothing beat a walk across the fells and I could do that on my own terms. In winding up my locksmith business, I realised I would be making time for the things I loved. It wasn't just about growing The Paw Store, or taking on talks without feeling squeezed, but devoting my energies to the fundraising walks and events that had earned Max a place in a worldwide community. That was the aspect of our lives that made everything worthwhile.

'Boys, let's get some fresh air,' I said on rising to my feet and at once all three were at the door in readiness for a walk. As we were only permitted to go out for exercise once a day in that early phase of the pandemic, I planned to savour every step.

8

A World of Our Own

KESWICK HAS ALWAYS ATTRACTED TOURISTS. It's the perfect base for exploring the Lake District. At any other time, we could expect to see the numbers pick up before Easter and then climb into the summer. Now that lockdown restrictions were in place, the entire place appeared to be frozen in time. With hotels, shops and restaurants shuttered, and locals only venturing out for essential reasons, it felt as though we lived in a ghost town.

In that time, a walk with the dogs became the highlight of each day. With my work as a locksmith behind me, and with it the chance to stretch our legs while patrolling properties and grounds, I made sure that we made the most of our time outside. Before the pandemic, we used to jump in the van to venture far and wide. Now, we stayed local. At first, I had thought we would quickly grow tired of the same old paths. In reality, this proved to be a revelation. By staying closer to home than usual, it felt like an exploration of walks we had previously overlooked.

'Well, we've never seen the town from here,' I said to the dogs from a clearing one evening, having clambered up a steep woodland slope off the Borrowdale Road. Underfoot, the path looked like it had barely been used in years. With no traffic below, all we could hear was the mewing call of Red Kites as they soared on the thermals overhead. Paddy and Harry had trotted off to inspect the bracken, which sent a number of rabbits scattering.

I always love to see wildlife and during this time I wasn't disappointed. With so little human activity, it seemed like nature found a way to flourish. Even though we had seen enough red deer in Scotland to last a lifetime, it was a joy to witness them popping up in fields and even streets on the outskirts of town. Every time we set off for a little exploration, it made me keenly aware of the impact we have on this planet.

At such a challenging moment in our lives, a local stroll was a simple pleasure that I grew to love. The dogs also seemed to really appreciate the peace and quiet. With the weather on our side and no planes in the sky, we could lose ourselves in a newfound wilderness within minutes of leaving the house. Away from the news and worries about the virus, such a tranquil time with Max, Paddy and Harry left me feeling like I was in my element. Sometimes Angela would join us and bring her camera along. With her work on hold, it was great to see her develop an interest in photography and become really quite passionate about it. In adversity, it seemed to me, we had each found ways to appreciate simple things.

Then there was the litter. Before the pandemic, it had long been a bugbear of mine. Poor Max had cut his paws on broken glass on several occasions and I would always return home with a discarded bag or a bottle for the bin. I could never understand why people would show such a lack of respect, for themselves as much as others, and the fragile planet that we share. In the first few weeks of lockdown, a group of locals arranged a litter pick. Every day, we'd see people coming back with refuse sacks heaving with cans and empty crisp packets, but slowly their haul began to shrink. Eventually, the pickers considered the job done, just as we found ourselves returning home happily empty-handed.

'Doesn't it make a difference?' I said to the boys one day when we ventured to the lake shore. I was so used to spotting rubbish bobbing in the shallows and also grateful to Paddy or Harry for swimming out to bring it in while Max and I watched from the edge. Even so, it broke my heart to see them retrieve items for me that should never have been there in the first place. As lockdown stretched through springtime, however, the dogs would barrel into the shallows and then look back at me in disappointment because there was nothing to fetch. That soon changed when I took a ball for them. I'd also fire up my camera phone to capture the moment when they splashed in to bring it back.

'Go, boys! Show off your swimming skills!'

I really enjoyed making short clips on our little adventures and then sharing them with the Facebook community on our return home. I'd progressed from sharing snaps simply because the videos added a bit of variety and then made it a regular event because the feedback was so positive. It was also becoming somewhat overwhelming in terms of the viewing numbers. I knew that lockdown was responsible. So many people were stuck indoors and the stories some shared with me about the hardships they faced were deeply upsetting. At the same time, they had all reached out because of a connection with Max. Just seeing him, Paddy and Harry at play in the fresh air had become a beacon of hope at a dark time, so they told me. That was all I needed to hear to feel that what we were doing was worthwhile.

'OK, who's ready for a jetty jump?'

This was the moment that always seemed to bring out the best in the community. Max had started what was now a regular event whenever our walks took us along this stretch of the lake. Derwentwater jetties are quite a tourist attraction. There are eight in total that jut out into the water to serve the pleasure cruisers. They also make ideal jumping-off points and not just for humans, as Max was first to demonstrate many years ago when he launched himself after a ball I had thrown.

*　　*　　*

Max has always had a love affair with water. At a time when I was slowly expanding the boundary of my world, one street at a time, we had ventured down to the lake shore together one day. As soon as I let him off the lead, he was straight into the shallows and he wouldn't come out. Having spent most of his life in a yard, he seemed amazed at what he'd discovered. The only way I could coax him out was by throwing toys for him to fetch and then progressively tossing them closer to the path. I loved his passion for getting wet and when he took himself swimming, it was a joy to see. As for the jetty jumping, Max had invented that for himself. We'd walked to the end of one so we could admire the light on the water. Max was sniffing around the timber decking and I'd happened to find a tennis ball in my pocket. When I threw it in, I thought he would hare back to the lakeshore path and splash in that way, but no. Without fear or thought, he just leaped off the edge. It must have been about a metre drop, but he'd accelerated so hard off the boards that he sort of swan-dived safely into the water.

A minute later, having paddled to dry land with the ball in his mouth, Max was back at my feet, begging me to do it again.

Over time, the jetty jump became a regular feature of our walks. Sometimes we would attract quite a crowd. There's something so joyful and uplifting about watching a Springer Spaniel attempting to go airborne with its ears spread out like little wings. Max absolutely loved it, as did the community when I shared picture and clips.

Paddy was fourteen weeks old when he first followed Max off the jetty. He'd watched him with interest and his first attempt was more of a plop into the water. With experience came confidence, however, and after Max retired from such acrobatics it was Paddy who led the charge. He's just as strong and slinky in the water as he is out of it and ultimately that encouraged Harry to give it a shot. He was a little more cautious with his jumps, preferring the experience once he was in the water. It was then that Paddy seemed to channel his inner great white shark. I'd throw a toy for Harry, who took his time getting into the lake. He'd look at me first, as if seeking permission to proceed. Once he'd jumped in, the paddling would begin and that's when Paddy would circle around him.

To avoid a fight for the stick, I always had a spare one to distract the predator in our pack. In this way, we spent many happy times amusing not just ourselves but the online community. I'd film it without commentary, one of two clips from our daily walk I liked to upload each evening. Whenever we did the jumps during lock-down, the viewing count spiked considerably. It had nothing to do with the quality of my recordings, which were handheld and unedited. I think people were drawn to three dogs enjoying a moment of sheer freedom –

something we'd all had to forfeit for the sake of the nation's health.

One morning in May, I decided to take our walk to the other side of the lake. The dogs loved running around in the woods behind the bank. Plus, there were ball-throwing opportunities for them in the shallows. Throughout lockdown, the weather had been idyllic. The clear, bright skies and a gentle breeze made this world that nature was reclaiming seem picture-perfect. I couldn't forget why we were in this situation, but some-times moments like this could be bliss. As the sun had only just climbed over the fells behind the opposite shore, the light sparkled on the rippling water. It made for a beautiful backdrop as Max, Paddy and Harry splashed about, and so I pulled out my phone to capture a clip. Instead of hitting 'record', however, I accidentally fired up the livestream function.

'Oh, dear ...'

Up until this moment, I'd had no idea how people on Facebook seemed to broadcast in the moment. It was a rude wake-up call because despite fiddling around trying to shut it down, my phone continued sharing the scene to a worryingly fast-growing audience.

'I'm really sorry,' I said feebly, aware that people were watching. 'I seem to have pressed the wrong button.'

Frantically, I had another go at closing down the broadcast. At the same time I realised that I was point-ing the camera at the ground, which made me look even more out of control. So, I found the dogs in the frame and decided to just ride it out.

'Good morning, everyone. It's a beautiful day here in the Lake District and here we are on our once-a-day walk, having a splash about …'

I don't recall exactly how I narrated the moment. I worried that I was making myself look like a complete fool. I didn't know what else to do but just go with it. Even when I finally worked out how to stop the livestream, I couldn't see any way to save it as a video clip. So, I just pocketed my phone, thinking I had wasted a good opportunity and went back to enjoying the walk.

'Never mind, eh?' I said to the boys. 'I don't suppose many people noticed.'

Back home, on checking in with Max's Facebook community page, I took one look at the number of hits the livestream had earned and felt completely mortified. I thought twenty or so people might have seen my accidental broadcast. In fact, thousands had viewed it. My first instinct was to delete it on account of the shaky start. Then I watched it for myself, smiling as Harry splashed into the water to join Paddy while Max just stood in the shallows, looking happy.

'Shall we leave it up?' I asked them, but I didn't need a reply even if they could speak. 'We'll leave it up.'

The next day, almost 25,000 people had watched my dogs paddling around at the edge of the lake, which was when I started to view this broadcast function in a whole new light.

*   *   *

We were living at a time when we could no longer take things for granted. In the midst of a global pandemic, we found ourselves cut off from each other in difficult ways. We were forbidden from meeting friends or family. Schools and offices were shut. At every opportunity, we were advised to stay behind closed doors and that proved more challenging for some than others. This became apparent to me as I read through some of the comments under the livestream. People were posting from flats and bedsits or just urban areas with little green spaces. Somehow, seeing Max, Paddy and Harry in such a beautiful setting had transported them. In a sense, the dogs had provided them with a temporary escape. It gave them strength to see through their day.

When I considered what it meant to people, even if it was just a minority among the many thousands who had watched that clip, I knew we had to continue.

'All set, Max? Paddy? Harry? Right, we are live ...'

To make the films as accessible as possible for as many people, I aimed to broadcast to the Facebook community at the same time each day. We didn't do anything special or different from our regular routine, we just went out for our designated daily exercise and I hit that magic button.

'Good morning, everyone. It's another beautiful and sunny day so we thought we'd climb up to Latrigg. We're high enough now to see over the rooftops behind us and if we keep going to where the path turns, we should get a lovely view of the River Derwent.'

We did nothing out of the ordinary. There was no polished introduction, nor did I dress up for the occasion. Paddy would lope ahead and seek out sticks, while Max toddled along beside me and Harry watched over him like the caring soul he has always been. We never ventured beyond Max's comfort zone. I knew when to turn around so it didn't feel like a stretch for him and though we rarely saw another soul, we brought thousands of people with us in spirit.

Sometimes we shared a jetty jumping adventure. On other occasions, we'd walk up to the churchyard with a flask and enjoy what became known online as 'A Brew for Moo', which has always been Max's pet name. There, I'd sit with Max beside me and enjoy a cup of tea while inviting others to lose themselves in the view of the surrounding fells.

'Over there, just beyond that sheep field, is Castlerigg. When both of us were a little younger, Max and I would walk to the top and take a packed lunch ...'

We offered no plot, script or drama. There was little purpose to our broadcasts beyond the simple act of helping people to escape from their surroundings. Even so, with the world seemingly on pause, Max's Facebook community grew beyond anything I could have imagined. In a bid to be slightly professional, I brought a little handheld gimbal, which is basically a phone selfie stick with a clever stabiliser that cuts down on the wobbles. I even added a small microphone with a wind muff that clipped to the collar of my coat, which meant everyone could hear me clearly as I pointed out landmarks or chatted to the dogs.

Within weeks, as lockdown became a routine part of our lives, I found myself walking the dogs with upwards of 30,000 people from all around the world enjoying the same experience. For me, it felt like an honour and responsibility. For Max, Paddy and Harry, it was just time out in the fresh air and they knew how to make the most of that. Often, the feedback was from those who missed the Lake District and looked forward to returning at a brighter time, but the comments I watched out for came from viewers who simply enjoyed seeing the dogs on a daily basis. They represented so many things to different people, but it often came down to hope. For them, Max, Paddy and Harry brought everyone together, which is why I still livestream our walks to this day.

9

A Moment of Light

OUR FIRST LOCKDOWN REMINDED ME that dogs can be a lifesaver. Unaware of the pandemic that had practically caused the world to go on hold, Max, Paddy and Harry showed me how to seize each day whenever we had the chance. Even if that came down to one permitted walk, we savoured every step. And by inviting our online community to join us, I hope we helped to bring a little light into a dark and difficult time for so many.

'What a view!'

For so many people in the UK, that period in 2020 between March and July was absolutely horrendous. People lost loved ones, or were prevented from seeing the sick and elderly, even if just to hold their hands. In late spring, Angela's father, Alistair, was admitted to hospital with a heart condition. Finding herself unable to visit him had been really tough on them both. It had been a huge relief when he recovered, but that separation between two people who needed each other really hit home for me. I even saw it in poor Paddy. Whenever our walk took us to the car park where we used to meet Bella, I'd notice him looking around as if something was missing. If anything, it strengthened my determination to keep sharing our daily walks to help Max's community feel connected.

It wasn't just the livestreams that went stratospheric in this period. I had opened The Paw Store so I could spend more time with Max in his old age, with Paddy and Harry for company. With the closure of my locksmith business and the sale of my tools, I found myself with quite a bit of space on my hands. It didn't last long, however, for as the demand for Max-branded products went through the roof, I found myself filling it with stock. A few weeks after I had made the difficult and somewhat scary decision to call time on a line of work that had been so good to us, I was immersed in a new business that placed my dogs at the heart of it all. If anything, I was busier than I had ever been before. It was just that I loved every moment because it involved Max, Paddy and Harry. Down at the Post Office, which operated on restricted hours, I found they became socially distanced delights for people who simply couldn't get out much.

In a way, I felt guilty that for me, lockdown was a largely happy and calming time. The weather was wonderful, nature had thrived and I'd had a chance to step back from the world for a while. In some ways, it became an opportunity for me to reset and recharge. It helped me to look at the business I had created with my dogs and start to feel as if it was sustainable. Not only that, I realised, but it could also buy me the opportunity to plan the charitable events that meant so much to so many people. Lockdown had called a halt to the fund-raising dog walks, in which hundreds of people and their four-legged friends joined us for a stroll and a bite to eat. Now restrictions were beginning to ease, I looked forward to having more time to help Max's star shine even brighter.

It was when the opportunity arose to move into more space that it felt like everything was falling into place. As summer beckoned, we had begun to feel a little squeezed up at The Paw Store. Our turnover was so big that we could barely move for products awaiting dispatch. From hats to scarfs, gloves, T-shirts, mugs, puzzles and pens, all featuring his signature orange colour, I was simply trying to meet demand for products that helped people feel part of Max's community. So, when a bigger unit on the farm became available, we leaped at the chance to switch. This one enjoyed more natural light as well as space, and with the sofa installed, the dogs felt right at home. What's more, the new unit directly overlooked that breathtaking view we had seen from the back of the van on our first visit to the farm. All we had to do was step out of our new, improved Paw Store to admire the fells across the valley. I even installed the bench beside the front door so we could pop out when it pleased us. There, alongside Paddy and Harry, and with old Max resting his head in my lap, we could feel at peace with the world.

'Boys,' I said, one afternoon as the sun began to wane, 'let's never take this for granted.'

From where we were sitting, sunshine bathed the facing slopes of Lonscale. The way the bracken turned from green gold to ochre as it swayed in the breeze was mesmerising. Even Paddy and Harry had directed their attention that way, as if mindful of the rabbits that rushed for their burrows whenever we ventured over there. It was one of our favourite places to explore in fact, because even in the height of tourist season it could be quiet and out of the way. I also loved the gently rising slope along the top that could take us all the way to Latrigg and back down into Keswick. Below the bracken and rough land, a path cut across bare foothills in the early stage of a forest management programme. I knew the landowner was a keen environmentalist and looked forward to seeing how it would thrive as the seasons passed.

In thinking ahead, I was also well aware that a special date in the calendar was fast approaching. I smiled to myself and scrunched my fingers through Max's coat.

'Thirteen is quite a milestone in dog years. How should we celebrate?'

Max was content to bathe in the pleasant warmth of the sun while I sat there for a while, thinking to myself. Under normal circumstances, I would have marked his birthday with a communal event. As restrictions were only just starting to ease, and with no real certainty that they would until it actually happened, a big celebration didn't seem like an option this year. It was a shame. Not only did Max, Paddy and Harry love being around so many like-minded people and their dogs, it was an opportunity to bring in much-needed funds for charity. Previously, Max had raised tens of thousands of pounds for the PDSA. In 2018, he and Paddy had even earned a prestigious commendation from the charity for their fundraising efforts and work in transforming lives – including mine. As much as I would have loved to get another group walk off the ground to mark Max's birthday, I knew that it wasn't realistic that year.

'What could we do, eh?' I asked Paddy, who had come across for some attention himself. 'How can we make it a day to remember?'

*   *   *

I pondered the issue for a few days. It led me to think back to all the amazing times I'd shared with Max. Since he had come into my life in 2009, we had basically embarked upon one big adventure. It had started with very small steps. At the time, in the grip of chronic pain and depression following that traffic accident, I only felt safe at home. Max had given me the courage to just walk with him. At first, we ventured no further than the end of the road and then to the churchyard, where we'd sit and just be. Then, over time, our walks went progressively further until I could confidently say that we had a story to share from every hillside and mountain peak overlooking Keswick.

One year after Max came into my life, as a way of marking my road to recovery, we walked to the summit of Ben Nevis together. It was a huge and emotional undertaking for me and I couldn't have done it without him at my side. I went up as a man seeking to put a traumatic event behind me and came down looking forward to living my second life. Thanks to Max, I was still here.

Just as that climb had seemed fitting at the time, I started to think about a return to the summit as a means of celebrating a remarkable dog. I knew that he was too old to walk up Ben Nevis again. Even I had my doubts that I was in good enough physical shape to make it, but felt sure that Paddy and Harry would take good care of me. As I pondered the possibility, it occurred to me that I could still make this a shared event. I knew of a local business that hired tracking devices for running and cycling events. It allowed people to watch a competitor's progress on a website or app in the form of a moving dot on a map. Once I'd made the call and learned that it would be no problem, I realised I had the basis for an event that would involve the community at this testing time, raise money for charity and help celebrate the birthday of a beloved dog.

The only catch was that I genuinely could not guarantee that I would make it to the top. I was over a decade older than the time I had climbed there with Max. After months of lockdown and walks tailored to an elderly dog, quite possibly I wasn't as fit as I had been either. While I no longer lived in chronic pain with my back, thanks to a spaniel that helped me to return to mobility, it could still trouble me. Despite such misgivings, once the idea had taken shape in my head, I promptly made the announcement on Facebook so there could be no turning back. And when any doubt crept into my mind in the months building up to the big day, I simply had to look to Max as my source of strength and inspiration.

I was really looking forward to the birthday walk, but it wasn't just my uncertainty that I would reach the summit that daunted me. Max's Facebook community had grown so much during lockdown. With 120,000 followers, the charitable donations came flooding in. Once again, we were raising money for the PDSA and I was so proud of my canine team for inspiring people to support such a worthy cause. At the same time, I began to worry that if I failed to make it to the top of Ben Nevis then I wouldn't just be letting myself down. It was a concern I shared over the phone with Amanda one day. She and Rob had kept in touch throughout lockdown. Together with Adam and Lisa, we had all bonded over the joys of life with Springer Spaniels.

'Don't think about the outcome,' she advised me, 'it's the journey that matters.'

Max was snoozing beside me on the sofa. That year, he didn't just doze but went into deep sleeps on a regular basis throughout each day. I couldn't ignore the fact that he was slowing, or that Amanda's words of wisdom went further than a hike up a mountain.

'The first time Max and I climbed Ben Nevis,' I said, 'I wasn't even sure I'd make it beyond the foothills.'

'I'm sure Max knew you'd get there,' she said. 'He's always had faith in you, Kerry, just as he will when you go it alone.'

'Oh, he'll be with me.' I stroked his ear as we talked. 'I've arranged for Max to stay with a friend who lives nearby, but it won't just be Harry and Paddy by my side.'

'And how is Paddy?' asked Amanda, as she often did when we spoke.

She and Rob were still just as committed to bringing a puppy into their home as they had been when we met. In the same way, I knew that Adam and Lisa remained keen to breed Bella when she came into season again.

'Well, the romance is back on,' I said. 'Now we're allowed to socialise in small groups, Adam and I have already chaperoned them on a couple of walks.'

Paddy had been delighted to see Bella once more. Despite the ongoing jokes about marriage, they really did come alive in each other's company.

*　　*　　*

A short while after I promised Amanda that I would let her know when Bella came into season, I received a call from Adam. Not only had the time arrived, but he had a proposal that improved on the doomed car park encounter. It also sounded very sweet.

'Why don't you bring Paddy round for a sleepover?' he suggested. 'He can settle in with Bella and hopefully the magic happens.'

It was certainly a practical proposition and one that took away any pressure on them to perform – I just didn't like spending a night without my dogs.

'What if he runs away?' I asked. 'Or gets lost and never comes back?'

Angela was with me when I took the call. I guess she could hear the course of the conversation because she caught my attention just then and shot me a look as if to ask me to trust our friend to take care of him.

'Kerry,' said Adam, 'he'll be fine.'

When the big day arrived, I pulled up outside Bella's house and turned to address Paddy like an anxious parent.

'Behave yourself,' I told him, as Harry and Max looked on. 'Mind your manners and don't outstay your welcome.'

Paddy heard every word, but seemed more interested in the fact that the front door had just opened. Bella trotted out to greet us, while Adam and Lisa looked on.

Angela had advised me to drop him off late in the afternoon and not hang around, and I intended to do just that. She knew that otherwise I'd find every reason to loiter. I didn't want to leave Paddy, but I also knew it was the right thing to do.

'You can call any time,' Lisa promised me. 'And we'll keep you fully updated.'

'I don't need all the details,' I said jokingly, 'just the main headline.'

That evening, while Harry and Max made the most of the extra basket by flopping between the three, I found that I could barely sit still.

'What if he's homesick?' I asked Angela. 'Or off his food?'

'Don't worry, Kerry,' Angela reassured me. She had been scrolling through photographs taken that day. Having voiced every concern that entered my head since she'd opened the gallery on her phone, this was the moment she gave up on it. 'He's probably having the time of his life.'

When my phone pinged, I snatched it from the sofa arm as if it was about to take flight.

'It's from Adam,' I said, scrambling to open the message. 'Oh!'

It was a simple message, accompanied by a picture of both dogs in a basket. They were lying somewhat primly beside each other, looking like they'd turned in for the night.

No joy

On the one hand, I was relieved to see Paddy hadn't run away. On the other, it was disappointing to face the reality of the situation.

Over the course of the next half an hour, I did well to resist the urge to grab my van keys and go and collect him. Instead, I sat in front of the television with Angela without any awareness of what we were watching. Then my phone pinged once again and I realised I hadn't put it down since the last message.

It's on!

This time, I responded by speed dialling Adam.

'Success?'

'We hope so,' he replied. 'They went out into our back garden about ten minutes ago, which is on a slope. Paddy hopped on and together, they sort of ended up pinned to the fence at the bottom. It gave him the final push that he needed.'

At any other time, I would have chuckled at the picture he'd just painted. Instead, I faced Angela in delight.

'Are they OK?' I asked, having reminded myself that I was still on a call.

'Absolutely fine,' Adam promised me.

'Are you sure? I can pick him up now if it's all over.'

'There's no need,' he said. 'In fact, let me send you another picture to put your mind at rest.'

I closed the call and opened up our message thread. When the picture popped in, I gasped in surprise and felt all my worries lift away. It confirmed that Bella and Paddy were back in the house. This time, however, they hadn't returned to the basket to curl up politely beside each other. Instead, both dogs had hit the sofa in a tangle and passed out on their backs. The shot of the two lovebirds with their tongues lolling and eight legs akimbo made me laugh so hard, I almost dropped the phone.

*   *   *

Three weeks later, a scan by the vet confirmed that Bella was pregnant. It was such uplifting news and I called Amanda straight away. In return for Paddy's services, Adam and Lisa had offered us the pick of the litter. As I had no plans for a puppy, I wanted Amanda to reserve that right.

'Are you sure?' she said when I called her. 'Kerry, we'd understand if you changed your mind. Puppies are hard to resist, after all!'

I had called Amanda from The Paw Store while sitting on the sofa with Harry on my lap as Paddy picked an old brown envelope apart on the floor at my feet. Max, meanwhile, was curled up beside me, sleeping peacefully.

'Honestly,' I replied after a moment. 'Right now, I couldn't wish for anything more. I know all the pups will be going to good homes because we only offered them to friends who own or love spaniels. It makes me so happy to know that you'll be among them.'

As well as involving our friends in the Channel Islands, with the blessing of Lisa and Adam, I shared Bella's pregnancy progress with Max's online community. The comments on each post were wonderful and just so supportive. Over the course of the next two months, as little Bella grew bigger and bigger, I could feel a sense of excitement building. The promise of new life is such a wonderful tonic. Whatever issues we're facing in our lives, it's a moment of light that we can look towards.

10
Back to the Ben

THAT SUMMER, THE DOGS and I found ourselves looking forward to two big dates in our diary. I had announced that our return to Ben Nevis would take place towards the end of August. Now that Bella was expecting puppies – and beginning to look like a barrel with a head, four legs and a tail – it seemed as if they might arrive very close to the same date. It just added to the sense of expectation, which was exciting but piled on the pressure as I couldn't be too confident that we would make it home on time.

'Paddy,' I said, as if to reassure him all the same, 'Lisa and Adam have my number. They'll call if the pups are on their way and we'll do everything we can to be there.'

As I said this, one morning at The Paw Store as I made final preparations for our climb, I quietly hoped that call wouldn't happen while we were midway up a mountain.

* * *

The first time I hiked up Ben Nevis, Max had acted as my guide. He plodded just in front of me, showing me how to navigate some of the rockier sections of the path, but never left me to track a scent or go exploring. He had been such a soothing presence and when we finally set off for Scotland, I hoped that he would brief Paddy and Harry about what it would take to get me to the top.

'I'm relying on you, boys. Let's make this the best birthday Max has ever had,' I said as we crossed the border. I glanced across at Max, who was sleeping on the passenger seat. Just seeing him there always helped to ground me, which I needed then more than ever. The fundraising continued to take my breath away. People had generously donated thousands of pounds in the short time since I'd announced the hike, but with that came a weight of responsibility. Even so, I was determined to give it everything I had. I glanced in my rear-view mirror and felt so proud to know that Paddy and Harry would shoulder that load with me while following in legendary pawprints.

The historic Highland town of Fort William sits at the foot of the mountain, which is where my friends lived who had offered to look after Max. I knew we were close when the summit loomed on the horizon, bathed in sunshine.

'Remember that?' I asked Max and then hurriedly wiped my eyes with my shirt sleeve. I just hadn't banked on such an emotional response on seeing that mountain again. The first time I had come here to hike to the summit seemed like a lifetime ago. It also marked the start of a grand adventure for Max and me. Now, twelve happy years later, we had come back to the Ben and it felt like that journey was drawing to a close. From the passenger seat, my beloved old dog peered over the dashboard. In the distance, beyond rolling forests and glens, the pale outline of the peak looked like a charcoal sketch against the sky.

He remembered.

*   *   *

'Has it got bigger since we were last here?' I asked early the next morning as I stood at the foot of the tourist path and peered up at the mighty shoulder of rock. All I could see was the first of many false summits, but just then Ben Nevis looked even more formidable than it had on my first visit. Beside me stood an old friend from Keswick. Victoria had moved here some years before to be nearer to her parents and they had kindly offered to look after Max. She had two dogs of her own, who were joining us for this climb. They were both the hyper variety, however, and had already made a head start. Watching them go, I felt very daunted indeed.

'It's just the same as it's always been,' she said. 'Kerry, you can do this.'

In that moment, I was seriously doubting myself. From the second I'd said goodbye to Max and promised I'd be back for him at the end of the day, I found myself carrying misgivings I couldn't shake. Harry had certainly picked up on it. He sat beside me, pressed against my leg, while Paddy mooched among the rocks, looking ready to take me to the top. Between them and with Victoria for company, I reminded myself that she had to be right.

'Let's make a start,' I said and once again checked that the satellite tracker I had taped to the shoulder strap of my knapsack was secure and flashing. It was a small, electronic box of tricks I had picked up before setting off. With the device activated, people could now chart my progress online in the form of a moving dot on a map. With this in mind, it was time we got moving. 'Let's do this for Max.'

As restrictions had only just eased, it struck me that more people than usual had come to Ben Nevis with the same day out in mind. It was busy, which never suited me. What's more, the first section of pathway is quite steep. Within minutes of the clamber, I could feel my heart thudding in my chest. Harry stuck close while Paddy scouted ahead and behind as if to make sure I had space. Even so, I quickly felt out of my comfort zone. I had about two decades on Victoria in terms of age and on asking to pause for breath, I really felt my age.

'I'm just going to check the tracker is working,' I said, pulling out my phone as a cover for this early break. 'Oh, wow!'

While the dot had crawled across a small fraction of the map, it was a quick glance at the fundraising page that told me where the real movement was taking place. We'd started out with about £5,000 pledged. Now, that number was on its way to doubling.

I was delighted by the upswing, which demonstrated just how many people were watching us online but I also felt a sense of dread. I had only come a short way, yet in that time it became quite clear to me that my fears about not being fit enough were beginning to play out. During lockdown, we hadn't got out and about as much as we used to. Plus, of course, I had modified our walks to suit Max in his old age. As a result, I now found myself with a huge weight of expectation on my shoulders and a serious doubt that I could conquer Ben Nevis for a second time.

Pocketing my phone, I glanced down at Harry.

'What do you think, buddy?' I don't know why I floated this question. Had he responded by turning around and heading back down then I would have followed him. Instead, Harry met my gaze for a moment and just sat there patiently. Paddy was stationed close to Victoria, whose own dogs had all but disappeared, but he also seemed in no hurry. Both spaniels were here for me, I realised. Whatever I chose to do, they would stay at my side. Then I thought about Max, waiting patiently for us to return, and knew what had to be done.

'Paddy,' I said, and smiled at Victoria, 'lead the way.'

It felt so strange to be hiking this path once more without Max. I thought about him constantly, which meant he was present in my thoughts if not at my feet. With regular stops, often instigated by Victoria because she could see that I was struggling, I would check the fundraising page and think of my dear old dog. With every step we made the total continued to climb and I put that down to Max. He touched hearts in a way that I could never quite fathom. Just as it had when we first met, I found that gave me the strength to keep going.

'You're not going to believe this,' I said to Victoria, several hours into our hike. 'The community have pledged £25,000 and that figure is still going up.'

'No way!' My friend stopped in her tracks. 'Kerry, that's incredible!'

'That's Max,' I said and for the first time took the lead up the path. With Paddy leading the way, and Harry still at my side, I began to think that I might just see the summit after all.

*　　*　　*

It was a momentous day, yet I felt conflicted. I was so proud of Paddy and Harry, but I missed Max terribly. With lockdown behind us, it was liberating to enjoy such freedom. At the same time, I couldn't help but notice that the path was strewn with litter and it broke my heart. It was lovely that people could enjoy this monument to nature. I could never understand why some would be quite so disrespectful. I picked up what I could, but with limited space in my rucksack, I found it hard to stay positive. Even as we closed in on the summit, I didn't feel the same sense of elation that I had on my first visit with Max. By then, my back was really beginning to hurt to the point where I worried it might give up on me. It was cold and damp, with little patches of snow underfoot. Even with some room at the top to explore, Harry didn't stray from my side. I had tried to encourage him to roam a couple of times, but he stuck with me. He had inherited so much of Max's sensitivities, I thought to myself, while Paddy had taken on his guiding spirit by continuing to map the best route over the boulders and stones.

'I've packed something to help us celebrate,' said Victoria over a stiff breeze and dropped her backpack on the ground to rummage through. 'Here,' she said and handed me a small pot and teaspoon.

'What is it?' I asked as she found a pot for herself.

'Fruit crumble,' she stated, like that was what everyone ate to celebrate conquering a mountain.

I didn't question her choice. We just tapped spoons to mark the moment and tucked ourselves in behind a rock to eat in order to keep out of the breeze. I had also brought some dog biscuits with me for Paddy, Harry and Victoria's dogs. It meant that together we could quietly enjoy a moment of rest on the UK's highest peak.

'This is for you, Max,' I said, saluting him with my pot. 'Happy birthday to an absent friend.'

Maybe I just needed the energy hit because when we set off back down the path I felt a lot more positive. I also knew that with every step I would be closer to being reunited with the dog at the heart of this day. It wasn't long, however, before that buzz gave way to physical discomfort. I had been taking painkillers for my back, but after a morning on my feet they no longer seemed to be working. A spasm crept into my neck and before too long I was back in that dark recess in my mind. As it hurt me to slide my pack off my shoulders so I could reach my phone, I stopped checking on the fundraising page. I didn't need to look at the tracker page to remind myself that people were watching my progress from all around the world. It felt like an extra weight and before we had even reached the midway mark on our descent, I was ready to jettison it. I didn't feel good; I was in great pain and embarrassed that I had bitten off more than I could chew. I'd placed so much pressure on myself, not just with the climb but also my ambitions to raise funds with this hike. All I wanted to do was slump on the ground beside the path and just sit there with my head in my hands.

'Harry, I'm finished,' I muttered. 'I'm sorry.'

It was then, from the corner of my eye, that I swore I caught a glimpse of a dog in an orange harness. It trotted up in the scree beside me and took my breath away.

'Max,' I said with a start, but when I spun around to follow it, the vision was gone.

From a few steps below me, Victoria glanced over her shoulder.

'All OK, Kerry?' she asked.

I looked again, blinking as if to process what had happened. Had Max been there for real then Harry would have welcomed him in an instant.

'I'm fine,' I said to reassure her. 'Just missing Max!'

I knew that I had imagined it, but even so the sense of his presence stayed with me. With Max close by, I had always found a way to overcome obstacles. This was no different, I told myself, and even made an effort to catch up with Victoria. As I did so, Harry picked up the pace to join Paddy and the other dogs: it was as if he knew that I was safe now and that filled my heart with joy.

*   *   *

It took us the best part of the day to hike to the summit of Ben Nevis and then make our way back down again. In that time, I experienced both despair and elation. Through my eyes, this was the mark of a great adventure. I had Victoria to thank for accompanying me and Paddy and Harry for keeping me safe. As for Max, when I set eyes on him again I wrapped my arms around him and *wept*.

'You never left my side,' I whispered with my face buried in his coat. 'Thank you, Max.'

Victoria's parents had been among the thousands who tracked our progress online. It meant that we found them waiting for us with Max when we finally left the mountain path behind. His tail started wagging as soon as he saw me and that was when I crumbled. As I wrapped my arms around him, Max nibbled at my sleeve as if to say *don't do that again.*

I had been so focused on getting back to him that it hadn't even occurred to me to look at my phone. It was only as the thermos of tea came out that I thought to check the fundraising page. The fact that I had a seemingly endless list of notifications and messages told me that our hike hadn't gone unnoticed. Then I reviewed the total we had raised and looked up in shock.

'Unbelievable,' I said to myself. 'Incredible!'

'Go on,' said Victoria expectantly. 'Last time you looked, Max had raised £25,000.'

'Which would be a triumph,' I said after a moment, before taking my phone and showing the screen to Victoria and her parents. 'Now it's almost *doubled*!'

It was perhaps the most fitting way to celebrate Max's birthday. In total, he had inspired so many people to donate that he raised £47,000 for the PDSA. It was a huge achievement and the largest single donation that they had ever received. Later that week, safely home from an unforgettable hike, I would host an online raffle for the charity to thank everyone for their efforts. I also took the plunge after Max, Paddy and Harry with a sponsored jetty jump. As a result, in the space of just six weeks of adventure, fun and laughter, not to mention the generosity of Max's online community, we broke the £100,000 mark.

The total left me lost for words.

Shortly afterwards, I was stunned into silence once again when the PDSA informed me that Max had been nominated for the Order of Merit, a prestigious honour generally awarded to service dogs. An 'OBE' for animals, it had been proposed that the medal should be bestowed upon him for 'providing comfort and support to thousands of people worldwide and promoting the positive contribution animals make to human lives'. Several years earlier, he and Paddy had earned a commendation from the charity. An Order of Merit was simply the ultimate in recognition. There could be no guarantee that the process would go further than this nomination, but it felt like the mark of a life well lived. Even in his old age, Max continued to climb to new heights and we all loved him for it. By rights, he had earned a good rest. In reality, with Bella due to give birth at any moment, I knew the imminent patter of puppy paws would be something Max as well as Paddy and Harry wouldn't want to miss out on.

11
How Furgus Earned
His Wings

FOR SUCH A PETITE LADY, Bella looked like she was set to give birth to a bonanza litter. At her last check-up before she went into labour, the vet predicted that she would have at least six puppies. Lisa and Adam were fully prepared for the chaos this would bring to their household and I had advised Paddy that as a new father, he had responsibilities.

'Be a good dad,' I joked with him on a walk one morning. 'Don't just disappear on her, you're a better dog than that.'

While I was still recovering from our huge mountain hike, Paddy and Harry had returned with the same energy levels that powered them through each day. I loved that about Springer Spaniels. As a breed, they possessed a constantly full charge that made it hard to feel down in their company. Max was just as happy to stretch his legs and trot along beside me, yet it was increasingly evident to me that his world continued to shrink around him. It would happen to us all, I kept reminding myself, and tried to focus on enjoying every moment we shared together. I found it hard, of course. As a companion, Max had always been there for me without question. Now, as a fact of life, I had to recognise one day this would come to an end – I just couldn't dwell on what it might be like when he'd gone. So, when I received a text from Adam late one evening, just a short time after our return from Ben Nevis, it came as a welcome relief to think that we would soon have something joyful to focus on.

Bella has gone into labour. We'll keep you updated!

That night, I dreamed that The Paw Store was overrun by puppies. They were everywhere; climbing up the sofas, causing boxes to topple and running riot across the floor. Poor Max, Paddy and Harry were outnumbered and outfoxed, and looked at me with pleading eyes as if hoping I could make it stop. That only happened when I woke up and hurriedly checked my phone. With no further message from Adam, my anxiety levels quickly encouraged me out of bed.

That morning, before dawn, I tried hard to distract myself during our walk around the streets of Keswick. We had a busy day ahead, with a list of packing and posting to be done. I also needed to return a call to the town council, who had left a message to say they had a proposition for me about Max. It sounded interesting, but frankly nothing could stop me from worrying about Bella. I was desperate to call and had to remind myself that as it had only just gone four o'clock in the morning, most people would still be fast asleep.

'Everything will be fine,' I told Max and I must have sounded less than convincing because he looked up as if to remind me that we were all in this together. 'I just wish we could be as carefree as the father,' I added, as Paddy made a half-hearted effort to encourage a cat to hop onto a garden wall.

After breakfast, the call arrived that I had been waiting for.

'Kerry, there are some puppies ready to meet you,' said Adam. 'Just brace yourself for a surprise.'

Leaving the dogs in the van, snoozing in their baskets with a brisk September breeze whistling through the driver's window, I approached the front door with my heart hammering. On the hurried drive to Adam and Lisa's house, I had stewed over what this surprise could be. With no guarantee that it would be a happy one, all I could do was remind myself to keep an open mind. I reached the front step, wishing that Max could be with me but aware that it might not be appropriate, only for the door to open before I could knock.

'Come in,' said Adam and his grin immediately helped me leave my worries outside.

As soon as I set eyes on the puppies, suckling from Bella, who looked content but exhausted, I found myself lost for words. I've always worn my emotions on my sleeve and this was no exception. In that moment, I found myself presented with new life. At a time when my beloved dog was reaching the end of his journey, these mewling bundles were facing the beginning and that reduced me to tears. At the same time, I was left speechless by the fact that these were the biggest puppies I had ever seen.

'They're huge,' I croaked finally. 'And just three?'

'Two girls and a boy.' Lisa was standing beside me with a smile drawn across her face. 'I know we were expecting more, but look at the size of them!'

Throughout her pregnancy, we had commented on how large Bella had become. None of us had contemplated that this might be down to the fact that she was cooking up baby elephants.

'They're adorable,' I said. 'And lots to love.'

*   *   *

Furgus, Mabel and Cora weren't just big puppies, they were bold. Every time I dropped round, I would find myself mobbed by marauding miniature Springer Spaniels. With every visit, they seemed to have further grown into their bodies. They were also louder, more confident and generally more joyful. At a time when it looked like we would be going into a second lockdown, they brought sunshine and laughter into the mix.

I was so bewitched by the arrival of the puppies that a few days passed before I remembered to return the call to the council. I had no idea why they wanted to talk about Max and so I rang back with an apology for being tardy and asked how I could help. When the lady explained her reason for getting in touch, it left me lost for words.

'Over the years, Max has done so much for the community,' she said. 'Mr Irving, we'd like to honour his charity work with a park statue.'

A moment passed before I could reply. I had called from The Paw Store, fresh back from a walk. Paddy and Harry were stretched out across the floor. Max sat on the sofa, waiting for me to settle beside him. What I had just heard blew my mind. Max was my dog and my best friend, I simply couldn't process how to think of him as a monument of some kind. It also sounded somewhat final, the kind of honour bestowed on those no longer with us.

'I don't know,' I said finally. 'Can I think about it?'

'Of course,' she said. 'Just let me know if and when the time feels right.'

*　　*　　*

'Steady, boys. Let's do this like grown-ups …'

A few weeks after the pups' arrival, we introduced them to their father. Max and Harry came along for the visit, on hand to show support to Paddy. It's always wise to be cautious when it comes to canine ice-breaking, but we didn't need to worry. As expected, Mabel, Cora and

Furgus were beside themselves with excitement at meeting my three dogs. Within minutes, they were swinging from Paddy's ears before turning their attention to Harry and doing the same thing with his tail. Both dogs stood there stoically and shot me a look that suggested they would be expecting extra biscuits for their supper. As for Max, he stayed close to me and sniffed the pups from a distance. They seemed to recognise the fact that he was several generations older and while they trotted across to say hello, they didn't treat him like a climbing frame. It was so touching to witness how the dogs interacted with each other, a real privilege. I considered Max to be the wise old man in the mix. I hadn't forgotten the proposition from the council, but this moment was about new life and that was something to be savoured. As for Adam and Lisa, they were so kind and welcoming throughout this time. They encouraged me to drop in and also share pictures and short clips of the pups with Max's Facebook community.

As a result, the three Paellas (a shipping together of the names Paddy and Bella) became star Springers before they'd enjoyed their first walk outside.

Mabel had a spark about her that made her such a lovely dog. She formed such a close relationship with Bella and so Adam and Lisa decided that mother and daughter should stay together. We also had mutual friends and experienced spaniel owners, who fell in love with Cora. They were also local and on choosing her to live with them, it kept the family bond. Then there was Furgus, the only boy in the litter, who I picked for our dear friends in Jersey. Amanda and Rob had been receiving regular 'pupdates' from us throughout the pregnancy and following the birth and were delighted on being introduced to their little lad via videocall. Furgus reminded me of his father in so many ways. He was bold, playful and even had that same rolling walk as Paddy that told me he'd soon be the coolest dog on the island.

We had a simple plan for the puppies. At twelve weeks of age, Cora and Furgus would head for their new homes and the start of what could only be a wonderful, rewarding life. For Cora, that began with a ten-mile drive in the company of her new family. Amanda had made arrangements to travel by car ferry from Jersey to the mainland and then make the long journey by road to the Lake District. She would stay for a few days, allowing us all to catch up, before making the return trip with her new puppy. Then, just a few days before Amanda was due to set off from home, our world stopped turning once again.

For weeks, the threat of another lockdown had been looming. Covid cases were once again rising and it became increasingly likely that we would return to the restrictions that minimised exposure to the virus but maximised the sense of loneliness and isolation that had affected so many. When the announcement came, at the turn of November 2020, Amanda called me with her plans in disarray. As a Jersey vet, she was permitted to travel for the purpose of animal transportation, but limited to a maximum of twenty-four hours off the island. After that, a quarantine period would apply that nobody could afford.

'There's no way I can make it in that time,' she said on calling to work out what could be done.

'Then you'll just have to fly Furgus home,' I said jokingly.

Amanda didn't reply for a moment. From down the line, I could practically hear her thinking things through.

'Kerry,' she said finally, 'where's your nearest airport?'

*　　*　　*

Later that week, working within the restrictions that had just come into place, we embarked upon our madcap plan to deliver a puppy to his forever home.

'Buckle up, Furgus,' I said after Lisa and Adam had dropped him off at The Paw Store. 'You're about to join an exclusive club.'

It had been an emotional farewell. The puppies were only a couple of months old and yet they had earned the love and affection of everyone around them. Keeping our distance, I took Furgus into my arms and promised the couple that he was in safe keeping. I then placed him in the care of Max, Paddy and Harry, who had become quite familiar with this playful scrap and then checked my watch for the final time.

'We leave in five minutes,' I told them. 'Is everyone clear on the brief?'

From the seating area of The Paw Store, four dogs cocked their heads inquisitively at me. They had no clue, I realised, and indeed even if I could explain it to them, I doubted they would believe me. I certainly hadn't when Amanda pitched me her plan.

'A private jet?' I had said incredulously when she called me back soon after my joke about taking to the skies. 'Either you're a millionaire or out of your mind!'

'Neither,' said my veterinary friend, laughing. 'I made some calls and found a flight out, bringing three working sheepdogs back to the island.'

'And you thought you could hitch a ride?' I asked, admiring her ambition.

'We'll see you at Blackpool Airport,' she told me.

'Blackpool?' I said, unaware that the seaside resort just under 100 miles south from Keswick even had such a facility. 'Well, that beats a donkey ride on the beach!'

'Most small independent airports have closed,' she explained. 'This one is our only hope.'

'Then let's go.'

Feeling suddenly quite fired up by the plan, I had grabbed a pen to write down the details.

'Just tell Furgus not to get ideas above his station,' she requested. 'This is an emergency measure!'

Leaving little time before the plane's arrival – because restrictions wouldn't allow us to turn up early for the exchange – we set off in the van. I was following the sat nav because even though Amanda had told me where she would be landing, I still struggled to believe that Blackpool even had an airport. Once again, as we followed almost-empty roads, it seemed as if we had the Lake District to ourselves. It felt odd and almost uncomfortable. It didn't help that as soon as I'd strapped Furgus into the passenger seat with a special puppy harness he had started crying his head off.

'Everything's going to be OK,' I said to soothe him and rested my hand on his paw. 'I know it's a big change but Amanda, Rob and Archie will look after you. I promise you're going to love this new life!'

Furgus responded with another heartbreaking howl and I felt terrible. Through his eyes I had taken him away from his mum and two sisters. Now I'd bundled him into a van on some mystery journey with no sign of life and no doubt he felt very small and alone. I glanced in my rear-view mirror: Max, Paddy and Harry were settled quietly in their baskets, which when I decided to pull over.

The moment I placed him in the basket with his dad, Furgus fell quiet. Paddy sniffed his head, licked his ear to welcome him and then the pair snuggled together. It was a beautiful moment and also somewhat wrenching because I knew that I was going to miss this little guy.

As part of the arrangements, Amanda had sent me a letter of authorisation. In her capacity as a vet, she was permitted to oversee the transportation of pets. As long as the jet took off for its return flight within sixty minutes of landing, we were operating within the law. Even so, I didn't feel that confident when we pulled up in front of a security barrier at the airfield. I was happily surprised to find it existed, though we had been instructed to arrive not at the main entrance but an emergency access route. It felt like we were sneaking in through a side door and suddenly seemed so shady.

'Let me do the talking,' I said to the boys as a security guard approached my window.

As the guy read the letter in silence, I glanced nervously at Max. Despite the legitimacy of what we were doing, I still felt like some kind of Springer Spaniel smuggler. I only remembered how to breathe when he waved us through.

'Park on the apron,' he told me, pointing to a large turning circle where the runway ended in front of the main building. 'And don't leave the vehicle until the jet lands.'

I nodded casually, like we did this kind of thing every day, and then trundled towards our designated spot.

'This is weird,' I said out loud as Harry joined Max to see what on earth we were doing. 'No funny business, OK? We're probably being watched.'

Cranking the handbrake into position, I killed the engine and looked around. Apart from the sound of seagulls, there was no other sign of life. By now, both Paddy and Furgus had stirred. As Paddy stationed himself at the rear window, his little boy clambered across to sit in my lap. There, he placed his front paws on the steering wheel so he could peer out through the windscreen. We were hardly going to compete with air traffic control's flight radar, but when a dot appeared on the horizon minutes after we had arrived, the dogs kicked off to alert me to the incoming aircraft.

It felt like we were on a film set when the jet touched down. By then, another vehicle transporting the three sheepdogs had joined us. With Paddy on my lap as well as Furgus, we watched this sleek little aircraft taxi towards us. As instructed, we remained in the vehicle until the jet's fuselage door opened from the inside and the stairs extended to the tarmac. I smiled to myself when an attendant in a high-vis jacket ran out to place a strip of red carpet in front of the final step.

'Max? Paddy? Harry? Let's not take notes.'

Amanda was first to appear out of the aircraft. With the wind blowing through her auburn hair, she looked around, saw the van and grinned at the fact that this outlandish plan had come together. In response, little Furgus began to wag his tail with such enthusiasm I thought he might take off of his own accord.

136

LEFT: With mutual admiration, our future Queen and Max share a very special moment in Keswick Market Square.

BELOW: Max understood the assignment, Paddy was expecting a treat, Harry played it cool. One of our greatest honours, meeting the Duke and Duchess of Cambridge.

A raft of emotions just seeing the Brew For Moo road sign and for the crowds that came to support our cause.

A hot summer's day, taking in the view from Tewet Tarn. The orange army arrived in their hundreds.

Max looked after Harry as a puppy and Harry gave Max so much support in his final days. I started to realise that my boy was aging and slowing down.

ABOVE: How I will always remember Max: his lust for life and him flying off any protrusion to get into the water. Fly high, Moo.

LEFT: The emotional ascent of Ben Nevis, with the mental and physical struggle of getting back down shortly to follow.

BELOW: A very special reunion with Max after climbing Ben Nevis. He gave comfort and strength to so many. I miss rubbing those ears.

LEFT: A very special moment with Bella and her beautiful pups; such a caring mother.

BELOW: Paddy has had to get used to being used as a climbing frame by Miss Cora, Miss Mabel and Master Furgus. He's devoted to Bella and such a great father to his family.

Max and the bronze community-funded statue 'Max The Miracle Dog', supported by Paddy and Harry. A place to sit and reflect on what our boy gave.

The creation of Memory Wood in a stunning location on Lonscale Fell. The perfect resting place for Max.

No matter where we went, Max would patiently wait for me, tail wagging with the purest love and devotion that only a dog can give.

Max was great at conversation and an amazing listener, but he would always voice his opinion. He had a skill in bringing so many together.

ABOVE: Max, Harry and Paddy exploring the fells overlooking Thirlmere, one of our favourite places.

LEFT: Paddy taking a moment. I can still visualise the respect Paddy gave to Max; the bond they had was incredible.

LEFT: Harry and Paddy handing over a cheque to some of the incredible team at the Great North Air Ambulance Service.

BELOW: Hidden in plain sight, the Powered By Max critical care car outside the Pawstore just before handover. I'm so proud that Max continues to help save lives every day.

The arrival of Tally! So many adventures await this special little boy.

'It's time,' I said, waving at Amanda. It was so good to see her and I felt nothing but delight in knowing that we had made this work under challenging circumstances. Even so, I was struck by how much I was going to miss the little chap in my lap.

'Be a good boy, Furgus,' I said and blinked to regain my composure. 'Now go and make a difference to the world.'

12

'That's a Nice Pen'

IT'S AMAZING HOW MUCH QUIETER the world becomes without puppies. With a second lockdown in place, I found myself without distraction. It gave me the time I treasured most of all with my dogs for company. We were busier than ever at The Paw Store, while our livestreamed walks became a daily fixture that continued to help people find an escape from the restrictions that governed us once more. And I also had the space to be present in each and every moment with Max and that was something I valued more than anything else.

Furgus, Mabel and Cora had their whole lives ahead of them and it had been a pleasure to witness them scamper forth. Without the joyful chaos they left in their wake, I looked at Max, well aware that his best days were behind him. As the weeks and months passed, he continued to slow down. His joints became stiffer and our walks became little more than a leg stretch. Paddy and Harry were so good with him – they seemed to understand that I had to put his needs first. We often chose a favourite ramble along a lakeside track. It allowed Max to trot along beside me while the other two had plenty of scope for adventure from the wooded slopes to the banks beside the water.

To the sound of blackbirds and wrens singing from the trees, I would enjoy their company while reflecting on how far Max and I had come together. He really was a remarkable dog, who had brought hope and inspiration to so many lives. Naturally, I wanted to celebrate that. I still couldn't believe that he was being considered for an Order of Merit by the PDSA, while the council's proposition hovered in my thoughts. A statue was a lovely idea and a huge honour, I just wanted to be sure that if it went ahead then it would be done properly. I worried that it was the sort of thing that could quickly become ignored, or fall into neglect, and that was the last thing I wanted for Max.

'Can I make a suggestion?' I asked when the lady from the council called to follow up on our conversation. She had proposed that the statue would be situated in Fitz Park, a beautiful open space in town that runs alongside the river. Having seen it underwater during the flooding of 2015, however, when water poured off the surrounding mountains after Storm Desmond and burst the banks, it felt like a vulnerable spot. 'How about Hope Park?' I said instead.

I had been giving the location a great deal of thought. Keswick is lucky enough to be home to two parks.

They're both beautiful spaces, but in my view Fitz Park has always been the more popular of the two. It's also bigger and hosts more communal events, like cricket and the local parkrun. Hope Park is a much smaller space and lies between the town centre and Derwentwater. People often cut through it on their way to the edge of the lake, but I've always thought that the winding paths and cultivated beds offer the perfect setting for a little stroll or a moment of peace and quiet. Above all, I was drawn by the park's name: Max had given hope to so many and this seemed like a fitting place to honour his life's work.

'Well,' said the lady from the council, who seemed surprised by my nominated location, 'I'll have to consult with colleagues first.'

'Take your time,' I said, suddenly all the more determined that Max's statue should support what might be considered the underdog of the two parks. 'We're in no rush.'

As well as being in lockdown, which prevented any real progress on the creation of a statue, I didn't want to be drawn from the bubble in which I found myself with my dogs. I was happy there and content to be spending my days in their company at home, on the fells or in The Paw Store. Every day, in sharing our walks with the community, it felt like Max, Paddy and Harry continued to make a difference. I didn't want that to end just because Max was in his senior years but I had to make sure that everything we did was appropriate for him and that above all, he enjoyed it. His welfare was my priority, as it had been from the moment I found him in that yard. While the hike up Ben Nevis on his birthday had been a fitting way for Max to raise money for the PDSA, I had paid a price for the physical undertaking. I was still aching and tired, weeks after the event, so rather than think up bigger and bolder fundraising adventures, I made a deal with the dogs.

'When this lockdown finally comes to an end,' I said one day in The Paw Store, 'let's go back to what we do best.'

Harry had been paying most attention and responded with a quizzical tip of his head. Paddy slipped off the sofa to nudge my hand, as if hoping that a tennis ball might materialise from it. Max just gazed into my eyes and I knew he understood.

'A sponsored walk,' I said, for the benefit of the other two dogs. 'We'll invite anyone from the community who wants to join us for a lovely ramble. It'll be just like the old days. We don't have to go far. We'll make it open to all abilities and by starting and finishing at the same place, we can finish with tea and cakes. This time, we'll aim to raise more funds for a worthwhile cause than ever before.' I paused there and returned my attention to Max. He had led so many community walks, raising money for charity with every step he made, but I knew this wasn't feasible for him anymore. Even so, I knew he'd still want to be at the heart of the event. Just being there when everyone set off and then welcoming them back would be something he enjoyed while bringing happiness to others.

'You can keep Alistair company,' I said, mindful that my father-in-law liked to come along just to be among people. 'We'll make it a day to remember.'

*   *   *

That year, with tight rules dictating how we could socialise, I found it hard to embrace Christmas properly. Ever since Max's Facebook community began to grow, I've always been aware that it's not a season that everyone enjoys. Unfortunately, for some it can feel isolating and lonely, and this was something we'd all experienced, thanks to the pandemic. Of course, Angela and I tried to make the most of it at home and the dogs always brought sparkle to any occasion. Even so, I couldn't help but look forward to the day when life opened up once more and we could all move on. It didn't help that the days were short and the nights long – darkness never seemed to be far away.

Then, one day in February, a light in our lives went out altogether.

My dear father-in-law, Alistair, passed away in hospital. He had been so brave throughout lockdown, living alone in his late eighties, but ultimately died from complications of the heart. We were devastated by the news and the fact that lockdown marked the final pages of his life. As his daughter, Angela had done everything she could to help him feel connected, but with restrictions in place that proved deeply challenging and upsetting for her. At a time like this, Max, Paddy and Harry came into their own as sources of comfort and distraction. They seemed to sense when someone was in need and would just be there for them.

Together, Angela and I faced the sad task of sorting through Alistair's belongings in order to clear his flat. It was such a raw and emotional experience, but among the tears we also found things to smile about. Ever since he welcomed me into his family, my father-in-law had always been a great collector of pens. In my former career working in agricultural sales, I always used to have a couple to hand, branded with the names of suppliers or feed products. One time, I was awarded a golden pen by my employers for achieving a certain monthly target.

'Ooh, that's nice,' Alistair said when I showed him and seemed to have such a shine for it that eventually it ended up clipped inside his blazer pocket. So, it came as no surprise to Angela and me when we uncovered a lot of pens in his flat. In that moment it seemed like some wanted to tell us a story about him.

'What does this stand for?' I asked Angela, having found a pen with the acronym GNAAS printed on it.

'Great North Air Ambulance Service.' She examined the pen, smiling fondly. I'd found it in a drawer, along with an old photograph of what looked like a public event involving GNAAS personnel in uniform. It was one of those group shots that captured a ceremonial cheque handover. I recognised a young Alistair among the civilians – he looked so proud and happy to be there. 'Dad was a lifelong supporter,' she added and proceeded to tell me all about the vital emergency work the charity carried out to support the NHS ambulance service.

I'd often seen the helicopters while out walking the dogs. GNAAS had three in total, according to Angela, which took off in response to call-outs in mountainous areas and challenging terrains. As she talked about her late father's commitment to a charity that relied on donations, and the lives they had saved over the years, I knew precisely how we could honour his memory. What's more, in view of the bond that Alistair had shared with him over the years, Max was the dog that could lead the way.

*   *   *

It started with a small announcement. As Alistair had been a familiar face at our fundraising walks, I felt that I should inform Max's Facebook community of his passing. In doing so, I suggested if anyone wished to make a donation then they could give to his favourite charity. Within a short space of time, we had raised over £22,000 for GNAAS and that blew me away. People showed such generosity and kindness, and all because an elderly man liked to join those who finished Max's group walks to enjoy a cup of tea and a chat. How lovely is that?

'Look who it is!' I remarked to the boys soon afterwards. We were out walking when the GNAAS helicopter buzzed overhead. Normally, I'd glance up at it without much thought. Now I knew what an essential role it played across the north of England and felt a connection, thanks to Alistair and the generosity of Max's community. Indeed, I'd already made contact with the charity about the funds we had raised. They were incredibly grateful for the support and I had the opportunity to learn in detail about the considerable operational costs involved in providing such a vital service. Without GNAAS, I was left in no doubt that lives would be lost. Every year, they provided pre-hospital care to hundreds of injured or severely ill patients, often having to answer emergency call-outs from challenging or isolated places like mountains and fells.

Here in the Lake District, our nearest trauma centre is over an hour and a half away. Relying on road vehicles, that could mean the difference between life and death. With a qualified surgeon on every call-out, capable of performing anything from blood transfusions to open-heart surgery at the scene, these guys were incredible. With my father-in-law in mind, I had promised that this first donation would not be the last. It gave me and my dear old dog a renewed sense of purpose. Together with

Max, Paddy and Harry, I'd stopped to watch the heli-copter fly on towards the horizon. It was amazing how far things had developed from the discovery of an old pen and it proved to me that with commitment, passion and kindness, great things could come from small begin-nings.

'We can build on this,' I told him. 'Max, you can make a difference.'

13

A Port in a Storm

FOR A LIFE LIVED IN LOCKDOWN, we had never been busier. When the council called with exciting news, I realised it was about to shift into yet another gear for they had agreed with my suggestion that Hope Park would be a fitting site for a statue to Max. Not only that, but in our conversations about what he represented to people, we discussed ways that the statue could also be a place to reflect and feel comforted by the spirit of his presence. As such, we settled on the idea of a stone bench. Not just one that served as a plinth for the statue of Max but also provided a place to sit for anyone who wished to feel close to him.

From that moment on, it was all systems go. The council appointed a wonderful local sculptor called Kirsty, who worked with bronze. She began by meeting Max at the park. I came along for the ride, along with Paddy and Harry, so she could see the Brown-Legged Gang in all their glory. Together, we found the designated spot for the statue. It stood to one side of the path just opposite a pedestrian entrance to the park. I could imagine Max sitting there ready to greet people. When I positioned myself there, I also realised I could see two significant landmarks in his life. If I looked up to the northeast, above and beyond the town's rooftops, I could see the churchyard where we would sit together on our first walks. That had been such a special time, when it felt like that lonely little dog and I drew strength from each other. Turning to face the southwest, as if following a line of sight from where we bonded all those years ago, I had an unbroken view across the lake. Beyond, the fell line rose to the summit of Catbells, which was the highest point on one of Max's favourite walks. It made this spot perfect, I thought, on standing back with Paddy and Harry so that Kirsty could take the first of many photographs of her subject.

'See how he sits so still,' I said quietly so as not to disturb her work. I turned to address Paddy and Harry directly, only to find their attention had been drawn by a squirrel on the railings. 'You'd make the worst statues,' I chuckled to myself.

A few minutes later, swapping her camera for a tape measure, Kirsty set about measuring Max from head to tail and shoulder to paw. She took the tape between his eyes and along the length of his nose and ears. In his old age, Max had developed a habit of slumping hard to one side when he sat. With stiff joints, it just seemed more comfortable for him so when he adopted this position for the sculptor we decided it was a characteristic that should literally be set in stone. It also reminded me what a dependable role young Harry had played in the four years since he came into our lives. Now, whenever they sat beside each other, Max would lean on him.

A couple of days after Max completed the first of several sittings, I received a call from the PDSA. Following his nomination for the Order of Merit, the charity invited people helped by Max to submit testimonials. Some came from the Facebook community, where most recently the daily livestreams of his walks had provided a means of escape throughout lockdown. Others were sent in by those who had benefited from Max's charity fundraising events. Combined, so the PDSA told me, it was enough to convince the panel that he was a worthy recipient – and I just wept.

With the statue in progress, and a medal in the post because restrictions ruled out a ceremony, I was thrilled to see that Max was receiving the recognition he deserved. I just worried that time was running out for him. I did everything I could to be sure he was happy and comfortable, yet we could all sense him winding down. He slept for increasingly longer periods and so deeply that frequently I would find myself resting a hand on his ribcage to be sure he was still breathing. For some time, I'd been helping him in and out of the van and indeed Max no longer looked like he could jump in and out, even if he wanted to. Paddy and Harry were so gentle with him. I wondered whether they purposely left a few extra kibbles in their bowls at mealtimes so Max could make the most of his routine clearing-up operation.

As soon as the sittings were finished, and all manner of measurements taken, Kirsty the sculptor made a scale model of Max. I thought the 'maquette', as it was called, looked amazing, but apparently it was just for reference. I had visited her studio to pick up a copy of a sheet of paper that Max had sat upon so that she could draw around him. The outline would effectively match the base of the finished statue and I had been tasked with commissioning the plinth that it would sit upon.

'It's hard-hat time,' I told the boys as we pulled off the mountain pass and parked in front of a cluster of stone walled buildings with sloped, corrugated roofs. 'For me, perhaps, if not for you guys.'

Nestled between huge shoulders of rock near Borrowdale, Honister Slate Mine has been in operation for centuries. It's a popular tourist attraction, but remains fully operational. I had come here because I wanted the bench to be as solid and enduring as Max himself. Having called to explain what I had in mind, they suggested that I visit to view a slab that might fit the bill.

I had assumed the slab in question had been extracted and polished. Instead, shortly after finding the guy I had spoken to over the phone, I was invited to jump into a Land Rover with the dogs.

'Where are we going?' I asked as he spun the vehicle towards a dirt track.

Max, Paddy and Harry didn't seem to care. They looked thrilled to be rattling along on a new adventure. Our driver grinned and gestured towards the point where the track met the ridge line.

When we crested the ridge and the mine entrance came into view, I had assumed we would stop. Instead, holding onto my hard hat, we drove straight in. The tunnel was shored and illuminated, and large enough for a gravel truck to come and go. It took me a moment to come to terms with the scale, but as we carried on driving I couldn't get over how deep into the mountain we were travelling. Eventually, after a couple of miles since the dogs and I last saw daylight, we arrived in a huge, illuminated cavern. When our driver pulled up, Paddy and Harry looked primed to go for a walk. With safety in mind, even though I knew Max wouldn't go far, I kept all three of them on leads.

'As soon as we found this seam,' said our driver and guide, 'we thought of your dog.'

Next, he led me towards a section of the cavern wall that had recently been blasted. Great hunks of slate were propped up on each side. I set eyes on the slab he had in mind before he'd even rested his hand on it. At roughly six-foot long by three across, asymmetrical in shape and rough around the edges where it had been mined, I knew that we had found the bench. It looked solid, handsome

153

and fit for all seasons. Unfolding the paper tracing from my pocket, I laid it on top of the slab. Then I looked across at my old dog and grinned.

'Max, this has your name all over it.'

* * *

With the sittings complete, and the sculptor hard at work in her studio for the next few months, my focus turned to ways that we could raise funds for GNAAS. In the wake of Alistair's passing, it felt like a cause that Max could embrace in his honour. The charity was dedicated to providing support to people at a critical time and in so many ways that had always been Max's mission. In the past, I would have planned a sponsored walk, shared it with the Facebook community and looked forward to seeing my dear old dog lead hundreds of people for a couple of miles around our beautiful Cumbrian landscape. But it wasn't only lockdown that led me to park the idea instead. The reality was that Max needed support of his own. It wasn't simply a question of winding in our daily walks, or helping him into the van or off the sofa. I sensed he appreciated little things, like sitting beside me or watching Paddy and Harry as they played in the water. It was a sad, reflective time, but I learned to savour those small moments as Max did. I felt as if we had arrived at the end of a long, rewarding day and in that quiet twilight we could just enjoy each other's company. Ultimately, no matter how tired or frail he might seem, Max would always wag his tail when he was happy.

'We'll do something for GNAAS when the time is right,' I told him once as we sat together in The Paw Store. 'And when we do, I promise you'll be there.'

Resting with his head on my lap, Max responded by raising an eyebrow to peer up at me. Then that tail started thumping against the cushion.

*   *   *

'Morning, Kerry! A small parcel for you today.'

I had just answered the door to my ever-cheerful post-woman. As soon as she handed it to me, I noted the branding on the packaging and knew exactly what it contained.

'It's not for me,' I said as she made a fuss of the dogs, who had trotted out to greet her. 'This is for Max.'

'Something nice, I hope,' she said before turning back for her van.

'Something lasting,' I told her and wished her a good day.

Inside, having made a brew to mark the occasion, I crouched in front of Max and placed one of the most prestigious medals that a dog can earn around his neck. There was no ceremony or red carpet, no speech or round of applause. This was a lockdown medal, after all, hanging from a broad and blue striped ribbon. I scrunched his ears and stroked the crown of his head with my thumbs.

'Congratulations, Max,' I said and my heart swelled inside my chest. 'You're a good boy.'

I took plenty of photographs, of course. As well as sharing them to Max's Facebook community, I sent a selection to Kirsty the sculptor. Then I rang the PDSA to thank them and from that moment on, our day ran away with us. Why? Because the charity issued a press release to announce that Max was the first ever pet to receive the Order of Merit since its inception in 2014. As a result, my mobile did not stop ringing.

I gave one interview after another, by phone and video-call, not just to news outlets in this country but all around the world. That afternoon, several television crews visited to record pieces about Max. We filmed outside to comply with lockdown regulations and each time the boys put on the perfect show. By then, I was feeling quite exhausted. It had been a long day, both physically and mentally. Normally under those circum-stances, I am quick to shed a tear. As we finished recording the final piece for a news station and then said goodbye to the crew, I was taken aback when the presenter was first to dab at his eyes.

'Do you know what?' he said with a voice that had just cracked. 'In this pandemic, all we've covered is sad stories. People have lost loved ones, or they can't see friends and family at a time of need. It's been gruelling and this is the first good news story that we've done.' He paused there to wipe his cheeks with the cuff of his shirt. Max must have picked up on it because he padded across to draw his attention.

'You're a wonder, Max,' he said, chuckling as he patted his flank. 'A port in a storm.'

14

Forever Max

AT A TIME WHEN I NEEDED to care for him more than ever before, it was so lovely to see the outpouring of affection that Max received as the story circulated about his medal. He didn't wear it all the time, of course, but whenever I placed it around his shoulders he looked so proud. Through 2021, as spring moved towards summer, I felt at peace with my dogs and the lives we lived. Throughout the second lockdown, Angela's passion for photography had really taken off. She loved taking pictures of the landscape and the natural world around us. With her camera in hand, she would often join us on our little walks. In a year when she'd been forced to put her hairdressing work on hold again, it was so nice to see her find a renewed purpose.

So, when it was announced that restrictions would be lifted at last, a small part of me felt sorry that we'd be leaving behind those quiet days to ourselves. I was in no doubt that the pandemic had been challenging in so many ways, but I couldn't deny that in the company of

Max, Paddy and Harry it had reminded me to treasure the simple things in life. It meant that as the world around us started turning once again, and the invitations resumed to give talks at schools and in the workplace, I made sure that time and space with my dogs remained a priority.

As the demands of normal life began to return, I wanted every day to be all about Max. I tried to stop worrying that each one might be his last and instead consider them to be a blessing. He was happy and in no distress; he was just a very old dog and there could only be one ending to that story as there is for us all. With this painful fact in mind, all I wanted to do was look back, knowing that I had given him the best life.

It took me some time to reach this outlook. First, I had to truly accept that Max would not be here forever. We all know that when it comes to our four-legged companions, yet it's only as they enter their twilight years that we're forced to confront it. Even when I stopped fearing that thought and found space for it in my mind, I still kept an ember of hope glowing that Max would somehow stay with us. Above all, I really hoped that he would still be here to see his statue. The way I saw things, it represented the sense of continuation that was always so important to me. No bronze could replace dear Max, of course, but I genuinely believed it would embody his spirit and offer comfort to anyone who cared to share a moment on that bench.

It meant that when the council called to tell me that the statue was complete and set a date for the unveiling, I looked at Max with a sense of relief as much as pride and joy.

'A medal and now a statue,' I said, before wrapping my arms around him. 'Who would have believed it when we first met, eh?'

*   *   *

One Friday morning in July, as dawn broke over Hope Park, the early birds who arrived to walk their dogs or exercise were greeted by a strange new feature. Whatever it was, just off the path in front of one of the pedestrian entrances, had been hidden under a large sheet. People certainly noticed it and some ventured forward for a closer look.

The fact that the sheet was bright orange provided the only clue. For it matched the colour of the collar made famous by the old Springer Spaniel at my side.

'If only they knew,' I said, peering through the driver's side window of my van. From the back, Harry and Paddy watched me with interest. The unveiling wasn't due to take place until later that morning, but having arrived at dawn to help oversee the installation I couldn't bring myself to leave.

Through my eyes, having seen the finished statue for myself before the cover went over, it *was* Max. Kirsty had done an astounding job – as had the guys from the slate mine – in preparing the plinth. Along the seam at the front was a simple inscription that had tested my composure: 'Max the Miracle Dog'. As soon as I stood back to admire the finished piece, I found it hard to distinguish between this incredible bronze and the living, breathing dog at my side. I felt such a bond with them both that rather than head straight home to prepare for the opening ceremony, I just sat in my van across the road from the park as if to keep the statue company.

'Yes, I know,' I said to Max, when I found him looking across at me with some concern. 'Relax, I haven't lost it. I just hope that your statue will connect with people as it has with me.'

I admit that I was worried. The last time the council unveiled a statue, a dozen people turned up. I had visions of pulling away the covers to only Max, Paddy, Harry and Angela, and only one of them was capable of clapping. All I could do was remind myself that when I shared the date of the unveiling with Max's Facebook community, the number of likes had soared. It was heartening to see, yet that was a global platform and this was a local event.

'Just keep an open mind,' said Angela. 'Whatever happens, you won't be alone.'

As well as the dogs, I also knew that I could rely on someone else for support. In fact, I rather hoped that she would steal the show. Several years earlier, a little girl called Sophie had come into Max's life. Back then, her mum – Nicola – reached out to me to say that her daughter had been struggling at school. She lived with dyslexia and that had rocked her confidence, but a connection with Max changed everything. Sophie had written a poem about him and it had won a prize in a local competition. I was so moved by her story that I invited Sophie and Nicola to join us for a walk and from that moment on, we'd become firm friends. Over the years, Sophie's confidence grew while her bond with Max had become unbreakable. When I climbed Ben Nevis to mark his birthday, she had even insisted that I carry her favourite cuddly toy – a little dog she called Max – to keep me company in return for a selfie with him at the summit. Now, as a young teenager, I knew she was capable of stepping up in public to officially unveil the statue. It would be an honour, I said when I asked her, and was delighted when she accepted the invitation.

I was hoping that Sophie and Nicola would be at the park before us so we'd have someone to talk to while we waited for the council representatives. It was only when the park came into view that I realised we might not be able to find them so easily.

'This can't be for the unveiling,' I said and took a moment to comprehend the crowd spilling out from the park and onto the street. The orange cover was still in place, while metal barriers had been placed around it by council workers to protect the space. 'Can it?'

It was Paddy who responded by pulling on his lead. Always the confident one, he liked to forge ahead, unfazed by anything in his path. As I reminded him to go easy, I felt a weight drop from my shoulders.

'Enjoy the moment,' said Angela, taking Paddy and Harry so that I could focus on accompanying the star of the show. 'For Max.'

Sophie was nervous. When I found her, it was clear that the sheer size of the crowd was proving to be daunting. Several hundred people had shown up. All I could see was a sea of faces. She was wearing her orange peaked cap with Max's badge on the front and had pulled it low over her brow as if to hide away. I was just as on edge, I told her, and then suggested that she spend a moment with Max.

'It's a big ask,' I said to Nicola as Sophie huddled in with him. 'If she doesn't want to do it, there's no pressure.'

Just then, Sophie giggled and wrapped her arms around Max, who had licked her face happily.

'She'll be fine,' her mother told me. 'Max will make sure of that.'

*   *   *

In some ways, I wished I had just some of the confidence that Sophie found in talking to Max because it fell to me to start proceedings. With a microphone in hand, I started by thanking everyone for coming and then acknowledged the amazing teamwork undertaken by the council, Kirsty the sculptor and the guys at the slate mine. Together, they had created a work of art under a veil of secrecy and now here it was under a cover of a different kind. My heart was beating hard as I invited Sophie to step up and reveal the statue underneath. I realised there was a lot of material for her to pull clear, but she did a fabulous job.

As the cover fell away, gasps rose up from the crowd, followed by the click of camera phones as people started taking pictures of what was a truly magnificent sight. Sunlight gleamed from the bronze statue of Max; a life-sized replica, detailed down to the waves in his coat. As everyone began to register what a true work of art they were looking at, the round of applause began to gather strength, followed by whoops and whistles of appreciation. As a finishing touch, Kirsty had even added Max's Order of Merit. I just stood there beaming with the real Max at my feet and with Angela, Paddy and Harry on one side and Sophie on the other.

'You did a great job,' I said, glancing down at my young friend. 'But you missed a bit.'

Sophie looked puzzled. With a wink, I took a corner of the cover that had fallen onto the bench and tugged it clear. The crowd responded with a coo and the patter of yet more camera phones activating. I watched Sophie register the two previously hidden slate blocks that supported the plinth. Each one was engraved with a name: *Paddy* on one side and *Harry* on the other. The two dogs that had supported Max throughout his golden years.

'That's amazing,' said Sophie, as one of the council representatives did a double take. 'It's perfect, in fact!'

'Keep your voice down,' I said playfully. 'I didn't actually ask permission for their names to be on there.'

Sophie tipped her cap back and looked up at me like I'd committed the Crime of the Century.

'It'll be fine,' I assured her. 'I thought it would be a nice surprise.'

'Are you sure they won't just take it down?' she asked and crouched down to pet Max as if he might need consoling.

I looked back at the statue and the queue of people that had formed, all waiting to take their place on the bench beside him.

'Bronze Max will still be here tomorrow, the day after that and forevermore. Whenever you need him,' I promised, 'he'll be right here for you.'

Part Three

Cradling my dear old dog in Manesty Woods, I rest my hand on his ribcage. Max feels as delicate as a bird, but behind those frail bones I can feel his heart beating. He's still with me, as he has been for so many years. I remind myself that he'll always be at my side in so many ways, yet in that moment I feel unbearably sad. That rhythmic pulse is nothing compared to how it used to be, but present nonetheless, which makes this so achingly difficult. We could just get up and go. Leave the woods and hope for another day. But I know that's not in Max's best interests and right now he is all that matters to me.

'Oh, Max,' I say, and stop there.

I can't find the words to express how I feel and to say how much he has meant to me, but then the strength of our relationship goes beyond that: Max just knows. I can spend hours in his company and say nothing because ours is a bond built on companionship. As I reflect on the simplicity of it all, he breathes out softly. It's a sigh and one I've heard many times recently, a sound we all make when we've had enough.

'I know, buddy.' I ruffle his ear. 'I know.'

A gentle breeze is blowing. It's nothing at all, but just right for this moment. For it reminds me of a chapter in our lives when the wind picked up as it famously can across the Lake District and lifted his ears horizontally. Paddy was with us at that time. Facing into the blast, the pair of them looked so funny that I captured it on video camera. I went on to share their 'flapometers' online and the rest is history. That little clip went around the world so many times it left us dizzy and served as one of the first times that Max brightened people's lives.

Smiling to myself at the memory, I rest Max's ear back upon his shoulder. The breeze lifts a few strands of hair, but nothing more.

Down at the shore, Paddy and Harry continue to explore. With their noses to the ground, they roam and sweep across the stones and into the undergrowth under the trees. They love it here, as does Max. He always has, which is why we've come to rest here ... and brought a friend as if to hand down knowledge of this special place.

'What do you think, Furgus?' I ask as another Springer Spaniel joins Paddy and Harry on the shore. 'At times like this, there's nowhere in the world we'd rather be.'

In response to my voice, the young dog switches across towards me and then double backs to run rings around his dad and sort-of uncle. Like Paddy and Harry, Furgus is so full of life and it feels like a fitting counterpoint. With Max still settled on my lap, aware of the love surrounding him but ready to go, I breathe in to steady my composure and then glance at the figure waiting at a discrete distance behind me.

'Thank you for being here,' I say to Amanda, who has also brought her dog Archie, along with a veterinary nurse, to assist her in making sure these final moments are guided by compassion. 'This is just how it should be.'

15

The Beginning of the End

THE DAY THAT WE UNVEILED MAX'S STATUE was one I'll never forget. The sheer size of the crowd who came to support him took my breath away, as did Kirsty's skill and creativity in rendering his likeness and character. People seemed to relate to Bronze Max as if it was Max himself. I watched as men and women, young and old, queued up to have their photo taken beside him. Some would cuddle up, or place an arm around him, and most would share a few words. Bronze Max wasn't just lifelike – that statue truly embodied Max's spirit and continues to do so to this day.

Bronze Max has brought so much sunshine to Hope Park. It's such a fitting location as well, because when Max and I first met, I was in such physical and mental pain that I couldn't see a future for myself. Max gave me a reason to get up and head out into the hills. He gave me a reason to live. And just as he did for countless others, he gave me *hope*.

In the days and weeks that followed the unveiling, I'd often find myself drawn to visit Bronze Max. At first, I went because I worried about him in the silliest of ways.

'It's chilly this morning,' I once said to Angela after our early-morning walk. 'I might pop down later and check he's OK.'

'Kerry, you're talking about a statue.'

'But he might be cold,' I'd reason, not entirely seriously but enough to factor a visit into my day.

Whenever I popped down, I'd take the three dogs and we'd keep our distance. I still love seeing how people relate to Bronze Max in quiet moments. Some like to just sit beside him and enjoy that moment of peace. Others make a fuss of him or even talk to him if they think that nobody is watching. Sometimes there are even tears. Small children are always fascinated by him. Even now, they clamber onto the bench to stroke and pat him, while anyone old enough to own a mobile phone often finishes with a selfie. Then there are those who simply pat him as they pass by – because who doesn't love a good boy? – and many rub his nose. It happens so often that a polishing effect has left the bronze with a shine that endures to this day and I think that's absolutely wonderful.

Bronze Max is there for everyone, no matter how they're feeling. He's become a landmark in Keswick and a tourist attraction for anyone visiting the Lake District. Best of all, his presence in the park continues to raise funds for good causes. As part of the installation, the council placed a collection box beside the statue. It's quite a handsome structure built from stone, with a little slot at the top for coins. The council hoped it might raise a few hundred pounds or so each year to contribute towards the upkeep of the pathways and gardens, which make for a sweet pocket of tranquility often overshadowed by the wide-open space found across town in Fitz Park.

Following the unveiling, however, the park keepers soon found that they had to empty the box far more regularly than anticipated. Thousands of pounds poured in through the coin slot and the flow hasn't stopped.

Since Bronze Max settled upon that bench in Hope Park, inviting anyone to join him, the council have invested in new pathways. They plant blooms in his signature orange colour and even commissioned a wooden bridge over the stream that runs behind the statue. The carpenter who built the bridge is a lovely Polish guy called Sebastian. Years ago, he used to work as a waiter at a café on the lake shore in Portinscale, a charming enclave adjacent to Keswick. I used to take Max there and sit outside the café with a cup of tea because the views were fantastic. Sebastian really took a shine to Max and I thoroughly enjoyed chatting to him whenever he served us. In fact, during the wintertime he used to sneak us in so Max could sit near the radiator even though dogs weren't allowed.

At the time, Sebastian was trying to get his carpentry business off the ground. His work is really good and I was happy to help put the word out. We lost touch after he left his job as a waiter to pursue his dream full time. Despite the years that had passed, however, I was delighted when I learned that he'd made such a success of his career and had been approached by the council for the Hope Park commission. When I took Max, Paddy and Harry to visit Sebastian's bridge, soon after it opened, I knew that our old friend had found his calling. It's such a beautiful structure with meticulous joinery. Sebastian poured so much passion into the project, but it wasn't until we crossed it for the first time that I noticed he had carved a patter of spaniel pawprints into the timbers underfoot. Even Max picked up on them, giving them a dutiful sniff as if he'd left them there himself.

Bless you for that, Sebastian! What a lovely touch.

*　　*　　*

The statue was absolutely one of the highlights of 2021. The fact that the unveiling happened just as the world emerged from lockdown seems deeply significant to me. We left our homes, blinking in the sunlight and feeling wary of being around other people. In Keswick, under Cumbrian skies, Bronze Max invited everyone to come together safely and reminded us all that no matter how challenging life can be, we are never alone. Above all,

I'm so glad that Max got to see himself immortalised in this way. Among my favourite photographs is a shot of all three dogs on the bench, with Max beside his namesake – it always reminds me that the difference we make can outlive us all.

That year, after such a long time with our lives on pause, it took a while for us to get used to the fact that things were returning to normal. The suffering that so many went through during the pandemic was heart-breaking, yet for me there had been moments in lockdown when the peace and tranquility really did seem priceless. I had Max, Paddy and Harry to thank for that. They took it in their stride and kept me company as I focused on making The Paw Store a business that brought happiness to me in the same way that Max's Facebook community pulled everyone together. Even so, as normality began to return, I couldn't ignore the fact that Max had declined significantly in the time we'd been in lockdown. I noticed it in small ways. Before Covid, we always used to pass hikers and some would recognise him. As the pathways became busy once again, I noticed people look at Max and take a moment to reconcile the very old dog with the online pictures and clips that had made him famous. Max still loved to meet anyone, but there was no escaping how tired and frail he had become.

We all grow old, of course. The difference between us and dogs is that they can't put their needs into words. It meant I had to pay close attention to Max and respect the fact that he needed more rest than Paddy and Harry. He still enjoyed his early-morning walk, however, even if it became a fraction of the distance we once covered. Normally, all three dogs would hear me padding downstairs and be at the front room door when I opened it. One morning before dawn, however, I found only Paddy and Harry waiting for me. Max had only just stirred, but as I leaned down to make a fuss of the other two while we waited for him to join us, he seemed to slip and fall from the sofa.

'You OK?' I asked and then rushed to him when I realised he was struggling to get onto his feet. '*Max!*'

With help, I encouraged him to stand. Gingerly, I let him go and he seemed fine. With Paddy and Harry locked into the routine that would see us heading out, I rose to my feet and Max duly followed. I grabbed my coat in the hall and then stood to one side with the front door open so they could file out.

And that's when Max fell over once again. With a thud, he toppled sideways onto the slate path and I went into emergency mode. Crouching beside him, I grappled with my phone and called the emergency vet. Max was conscious and trying to get upright, as I told the out-of-hours call handler who picked up.

'I can ask the vet to ring you,' she said, which was the response I had feared, given it had only just gone four o'clock in the morning.

178

'Please say it's an emergency,' I replied.

Ending the call, I scooped Max into my arms and decided to head to the practice anyway. It was a good half an hour away from where we lived. In a panic, despite the early hour, it seemed like the only place we should be. With Harry and Paddy in the back and poor Max in the passenger seat beside me, I tore along the empty roads. My head was spinning, unable to make decisions, and every time I glanced at Max, I feared the worst. He was just lying there with his eyes moving strangely from side to side.

'Stay with me, Max,' I urged him. 'Don't go like this.'

As we fishtailed into the car park, my mobile phone started ringing. I screeched to a halt, shut off the engine and took the call. It was the vet, who told me she'd just got into the practice.

'Where are you?' she asked. 'How quickly can you get here?'

'I'm outside,' I said, already heading around the van so I could open up the other door and collect Max. 'I'll be thirty seconds.'

Leaving Paddy and Harry safely in the van, I crossed to the main doors with Max in my arms. The vet saw me approaching through the window and was there to let me in.

'You've done the right thing,' she said.

By now, tears were streaming down my face.

'Please do something,' I said. 'Help him.'

179

Sensing my upset, and given the place was completely empty apart from us, she asked me to just lay Max on the reception floor. I crouched down with him, thinking at any moment the life would leave his eyes. The vet was so gentle with him, but also very efficient as she assessed him. It was on checking his eyes that she seemed to brighten a little.

'Max has had a vestibular attack,' she said, popping the stalks of her stethoscope out of her ears.

'What does that mean?' I asked.

'It's like a glitch in his balance,' she explained. 'And the good news is that it'll pass. At the moment, I imagine he must feel like he's been on a rollercoaster. I can give him some medication to settle the symptoms and he should be fine in a couple of hours.'

I listened to every word the vet said, but processed only one thing: Max was going to be OK.

'Really?' I said and burst into tears once more. 'I'm sorry,' I added, rubbing my eyes with the heel of my hand.

'You've had a shock,' she said. 'I suggest you take Max home so you can both get some rest.'

'And that's it?' I asked, upon which some gravity returned to her expression.

'The symptoms of a vestibular episode can be alarming for us and unpleasant for a dog like Max, but it isn't harmful. We just have to recognise that the vestibular system works closely with the brain so we have to understand what's caused it.' Here, she paused so I could read between the lines. Suddenly, it sounded serious. 'We can always run tests, but at the same time, we should recognise that Max is a senior dog.'

'I understand,' I said and thanked her as she excused herself to prepare the shot he needed. I stayed with Max, who fortunately seemed much more relaxed on my lap than when we had arrived.

Later that morning, once the effects of the injection had kicked in and with some rest at home, Max was back on his feet. I was so relieved, yet at the same time I had to come to terms with the fact that a chapter in my life was coming to a close.

Long before Max, when I was much younger, I owned a Springer Spaniel called Zak. He was a smashing dog and went everywhere with me. Tragically, Zak developed cancer without showing any signs for some time. When he did become unwell, leading to an exploratory operation, my beloved dog died without warning on the vet's operating table. It left me devastated. I just wasn't prepared and it took me some time to come to terms with the loss. It also upset me so much that I didn't dare replace him. Decades later, when Max pulled me out of a deep depression, he showed me not to dwell on the past or worry about the future but simply make the most of each moment.

It's just now we had arrived at a time when Max's quality of life was a concern to me. If his vestibular attack was a symptom of something more serious, and likely terminal, then at his advanced age I had to ask myself if I was doing the right thing in prolonging his existence. Was he unhappy, in pain or discomfort that couldn't be eased? Max had taught me how to be present with him and now I just spent the time fretting that I was keeping him alive to spare myself from grief.

*   *   *

Towards the end of that year, I was pleasantly surprised by the return of a friend to the Lake District, who also happened to be qualified to put my mind at rest. Together with her husband, Rob, as well as Archie and Furgus, Amanda moved from Jersey to live nearby. Having fallen in love with the Cumbrian landscape on previous visits, they had decided to start a new life here. As a senior paramedic, Rob took up a position with the ambulance service while Amanda continued her work as a vet from a practice just outside Keswick.

The family settled in so quickly that before too long I couldn't remember life without them. Together with Adam and Lisa, who had done a terrific job of raising Mabel alongside her mum, Bella, we often went on walks. Paddy was overjoyed to see the mother of his pups once more. They got on so well, as did several generations connected by friendship as much as blood. It really was one big, happy spaniel family. With Max's health in mind, I often just joined in for a short distance with him and, very quickly, Amanda picked up on my concerns.

'He's so tired all the time now,' I confided in her one day. 'Sometimes he looks at me and I can't help wondering if he's asking me to let him go.'

We talked as we walked, with Max close by while the other dogs swept out and circled around us. For them, movement was effortless and a reason to be alive. For Max, it looked like every joint in his body was aching. We'd been back to the vet on several occasions after his vestibular attack. She explained that it might have been caused by a tumour, but we agreed not to put Max through the distress of an exploratory operation. Whatever was behind it – and I recognised that we couldn't rule out another episode – his welfare was all that mattered to me. I just didn't know what to do for the best and that could upset me greatly.

'Kerry, I know you're doing everything you can for him,' said Amanda, in a way that made me think she was addressing me now as a vet as much as a friend. 'Right now, what matters is that he's happy. I can see that for myself.'

'But how will I know if that changes?' I asked. 'I can't bear to think of him suffering. Max has always been such a stoic dog, I worry that I might not realise!'

Amanda placed a hand on my shoulder.

'I'll tell you when it's time,' she said. 'That's a promise.'

16

The Making of Memory Wood

'BOYS, A LOVELY FAMILY will be paying us a visit so let's make room on the sofa for them when they arrive.'

Throughout the rest of Max's thirteenth year, it felt like we were on borrowed time. With support from Amanda, as well as family and friends, I sought ways to stay positive, not just for my sake but also for Max as well as Paddy and Harry. It helped to put lockdown behind us. From the unveiling of the statue onwards, I realised that as much I enjoyed the tranquility of that period, I had missed real connections with people.

Throughout the pandemic, business at The Paw Store had gone from strength to strength. Supported by an online shop, I was so happy to spend my days with the dogs as we processed orders to our own timetable. Our short little leg-stretchers were plentiful and we could take them whenever we liked. It also bought me time to focus on the fundraising side of our activities. Paddy's birthday was next on the calendar of events, early in the New Year. Traditionally, it was a time of mud and miserable weather, and so I decided to make it a belated celebration for the springtime. Announcing the event online, we looked forward to inviting anyone who wished to join us for a celebratory sponsored walk to raise money for GNAAS. I settled on a good route around a nearby lake, which I called the 'Buttermere Bounce', and was so pleased to see such a positive response to the cause. It gave Max's community something to look forward to and yet I had to give careful consideration to his involvement. While the birthday boy and Harry would no doubt have a great time, I recognised that it would be too much for Max. Also, I dared not think that far ahead for him. In effect, he had slipped into semi-retirement from public life. I knew it was the right thing to do, but it left me feeling so conflicted. People adored him. Of course, they understood, but it was a sad reality. What made it harder was the fact that Max loved meeting people.

Which is how the store visits evolved.

*   *   *

Ever since Max's Facebook page took off, I'd received a steady stream of requests from people who wanted to meet my dogs. As so many of members of his online community were drawn to them in search of solace at a difficult time in their lives, they'd often share their story with me. I'd hear from people who had experienced loss of all kinds. As Max, Paddy and Harry offered them respite, often in the simple form of a livestream walk in the Lake District, they felt moved to meet the dogs for real as a source of strength or simply to give thanks.

With The Paw Store open for business, I realised that I had a place where I could make that happen. It was also a lovely way for Max to stay connected with his community. As a result, at select times and dates the visits became a feature of our working lives. Often, people would bring treats for all three dogs, which meant they learned to respond to a knock at the door with huge enthusiasm. Having welcomed in our guests, I'd put the kettle on while the dogs vied for their attention. Then, once everyone had settled down, we'd chat about what brought them here.

And the stories people shared were heartbreaking.

With Max, Paddy and Harry at their sides, our guests would share tales of loss and bereavement that they would carry through the rest of their lives. I met all sorts of brave souls who had lost husbands, wives, partners, children and even grandchildren. The circumstances were often unbearably sad and I just hoped that as they talked, they found comfort in the dogs. At the same time, I found myself wanting to do so much more for them. I was touched that people felt able to open up in the presence of my three spaniels, but they still left carrying so much loss in their hearts.

'That was hard to hear,' I said to Max as we waved goodbye to our guests for that day. Harry and Paddy had ventured onto the drive as their car pulled away, with the occupants returning my wave. 'It must be so painful to live with such a loss.'

For a moment, I just stood there watching the dogs stretch their legs. We'd had a spell of dramatically changeable weather, with big, congested clouds sailing overhead and then suddenly breaking apart. As we stepped out of The Paw Store, it had seemed very sombre and gloomy. Then, as our visitors pulled away, a fan of sunlight swept across the landscape. It caught my attention and drew my focus all the way across to Lonscale Fell. The landscape management work on the lower slopes had exposed ancient tracks and patchworks of undergrowth. A scattering of sheep grazed on the ridge of the fell, which defined the rough ground in between. It mostly consisted of high bracken. At that time of year, it was turning from green to bronze. As it shimmered in the breeze, I saw only hints of orange. Mindful of the grief our last guests had carried with them, I focused my gaze through the lens of an idea that had suddenly taken shape in my mind. Then I turned my attention to the dog in the matching collar.

'Max,' I said, as Paddy and Harry sauntered back to join us, 'I think there's a way we can help people make that loss more bearable.'

Towards the end of that November, after seemingly endless rounds of planning, negotiation, agreements and permission seeking, I stood at the foot of a public bridleway to Lonscale Fell before an invited group of forty volunteers. They had come here from across the country, even as far afield as the US, to help me share a dream. Max, Paddy and Harry sat at my feet, which helped me find the confidence to thank everyone for their presence and explain our next steps. Many brought their own dogs with them. Some carried garden spades. Everyone had experienced loss, whether it was a family member, a friend or a pet, and found themselves drawn to Max's Facebook page as a small form of comfort. As a result, they had come together to volunteer their time and efforts in creating a space for themselves and others to reflect on sad times but also find hope for the future.

'So, we're here to plant trees to remember those we've lost,' I said and shared the story about how the idea had come to me as the sun shone upon the rough land on this fell. Since then, I had worked closely with a landowner passionate about the environment and called upon the help of the Woodland Trust to provide saplings and expertise. I was also no stranger to planting trees, having enjoyed many years as a younger man working for a forester. 'My hope is that we'll find comfort in watching them grow.'

I had been looking forward to this day for some time. It was a chance to invite people to a beautiful part of the English countryside and for us all to make new friends. We had connected thanks to Max's online community, where so many felt moved to tell me how much the dogs meant to them as a source of positivity in the face of bereavement. With the tree planting project in mind, I had reached out to invite them to help plant the first saplings. The response had been overwhelming.

With Paddy and Harry leading the way, and Max trotting along beside me, I set off with our kind volunteers on a twenty-minute walk along the track. When we came into view of the fellside slope that had drawn my attention from outside The Paw Store, it felt like a strangely sacred place. In the past it had been ringed by fencing, but much of this was dilapidated. We intended to redress that until the young trees were strong enough to withstand fraying by deer, while installing a small wooden gate that was open to visitors at any time. Historically, trees had once grown here in abundance only to be cut down for agricultural purposes. Now, we intended to create new life with a plantation and remember those we'd lost as it thrived.

Accompanying our little troupe was a man from the Woodland Trust called Peter. A lovely chap, he lived and breathed trees. He gave an instructional and passionate talk about our wildlife crisis and stressed how such ventures are the easiest thing we can do to help redress the balance. He had selected sapling varieties that were indigenous to the region, from oaks and silver birch, beech and dogwood to wild cherry and mountain ash. Peter explained how careful spacing would allow the trees to flourish while encouraging flora and wildlife to thrive at ground level. It was a fascinating and inspiring introduction to such a simple undertaking. When he finished, I felt like this was something more people should get involved in.

Then a morning of tree planting began, and with it, the chatter, laughter and some tears. Max, Paddy and Harry were on hand to provide comfort, as well as check that the soil was in good order with an enthusiastic sniff before the saplings went in. Once our work was complete, we had planted 150 young trees and made friends for life.

The planting was the first of many that followed and continues to this day with the help of a group of dedicated volunteers. Whenever people pay a visit to The Paw Store to meet the dogs and happen to share a story of loss, we can now give them an opportunity to let something positive grow from it by adding another sapling to the hillside. What was once rough ground on the slope of Lonscale Fell is now known as Memory Wood. There's even a sign on the gate made from local slate. It's such a peaceful place to visit. With the air filled with the song of skylarks or a simple breeze, you can just be there with your memories and feel like something good has come from a sad place. Voles and shrews have made a home for themselves there, which in turn attracts owls and peregrine falcons, and in the summer, wildflowers flourish that attract all sorts of insects. From outside The Paw Store, along with my dogs, I have been fortunate enough to see that simple plantation slowly taking root. Each tree has a story behind it. They form no particular pattern and are simply planted to give them all the greatest chance of thriving. Even so, in a certain light it seems as if a heart is taking shape upon the landscape.

17
Hurry Up, Harry!

MAX WAS ESPECIALLY TUNED INTO PEOPLE in need and his apprentice, Paddy, learned from the master. As for Harry, he seemed to have a sixth sense when it came to helping animals in distress. As a younger dog, he'd always be the one to come across stray lambs. Rather than become excitable around them, Harry would simply stop nearby and wait for me to call him. He's normally such an obedient dog that I quickly learned that there was a very good reason why he'd ignore me. I'd investigate and then find him watching over some bleating youngster stuck in a fence or caught in brambles. Once I'd released it or helped return it to its mother, Harry would stand down.

For a Springer Spaniel, a breed prone to bouts of extreme excitability, Harry has always been strikingly calm around other animals. I can trust them all implicitly off a lead, but Harry shines around them. In what is one of my favourite livestreams, I'm sitting on a bench with Paddy and Harry, talking to the camera about our day. None of us are aware of the ewe that ambles up behind us, pops her head between the two dogs and bleats loudly to say hello. Paddy is certainly startled but Harry doesn't blink – as if it's perfectly normal for livestock to make a guest appearance.

It isn't just sheep that my youngest dog likes to watch over. Once in Manesty Woods, I spotted Harry zoned out beside a stream. It was Max who always made a beeline for this spot because he liked to drink from there. On this occasion, Harry wasn't taking his turn at the watering hole. He was staring at something from the bank. When I approached, I realised he'd found a hedgehog that was struggling in soft mud. The little thing was absolutely fine when I rescued it and, once again, Harry didn't surface from his trance until his new friend scurried into the undergrowth. When it came to creatures great and small, this was one spaniel they could count on. So, whenever I called Harry and he didn't respond, I learned that it was time to mount a search and rescue operation.

*　　*　　*

One day in mid-December, we had chosen a walk along the riverbank towards the lake. The firm, flat ground was nice and easy for Max, with plenty of sticks to choose from as we ambled under the trees lining the bank. As we followed the course towards open fields, we heard the sound of barking in the distance. It sounded quite agitated, which I often treat as a signal to be wary. With Max in mind, who was too old to turn and run should we encounter a loose, aggressive dog, I decided we should turn and head back towards the van. It wasn't a big deal – we often take detours to prioritise the peace and quiet.

That evening, however, I learned via Max's Facebook page that a dog had gone missing in Keswick. He'd been out with his family in Fitz Park, only to be spooked by a loud noise from town and take flight. Worryingly, the dog had been spotted on the bypass, which was always busy with traffic. A few drivers had stopped, sensing the poor thing was in distress, only to watch it take off across farmland to the north.

What troubled me most was the fact that the lost dog, called Monty, was a Springer Spaniel. It wasn't a name that rang any bells, yet I hated to think what a frightening experience it must be for both the dog and his owner.

'I wonder …' I said out loud, mindful that the barking we had heard sounded very agitated indeed. It really bothered me, in fact, because in that family's situation I'd be beside myself. I looked across to my three dogs, who were winding down at the end of that day. 'I feel bad that we turned around now.'

Before dawn the next morning, after an unsettled sleep, I decided we should start our day with a walk around the area where Monty had last been seen. There are plenty of pathways around the farmland in question and we covered a fair distance while I called his name in vain. From the picture shared online, I knew Monty had the same classic tan and white colour markings as my dogs and was wearing a blue harness. That made him easily identifiable and once again forced me to register how distraught I would be, had I lost any one of them. I had also made a note of the owner's contact number, should we find him, but as a winter sun rose over the fells, we returned home without success.

Working in The Paw Store that morning, I simply couldn't shake off the feeling that it was Monty we'd heard. I tried to think where a scared dog would head if he'd raced off on the other side of the bypass. Monty could have gone anywhere, of course, yet I know the area well. Ultimately, if he'd gone north, away from the bypass, then the giant slopes of Skiddaw would funnel him towards the southern shore of Bassenthwaite Lake. As soon as I worked it out in my head, I realised I just couldn't sit and pack another parcel without checking it out for myself.

'Max? Paddy? Harry? Let's get this search party underway!'

It wasn't an area we often visited on our adventures. The lake is absolutely stunning and the surrounding wetlands are a haven for birdlife from osprey to curlew and plenty of geese. The ground underfoot can be some-what boggy, however, and so unless the weather was dry for long periods, we tended to go elsewhere. Sure enough, as we found a path it proved heavy-going. The ground was completely saturated, which wasn't fun for any of the dogs. In particular, I was mindful that Max's arthritic joints wouldn't thank me if we stayed out long and so I made the most of a quick leg stretch while calling out for Monty all the way.

'I'm sorry to say he's not here,' I said, trying hard not to think that something awful might have happened. The Lake District can be lovely, but not when lost and alone in wintertime, when the landscape can be harsh, disorientating and deeply unforgiving. 'Let's go home.'

The path back to my van took us around the edge of farmland. It was particularly muddy and I really didn't want the dogs getting mucky before the journey home. Max remained at my side, of course, and even Paddy found the sense not to stray far from the path. Only Harry decided that it would be a good time to explore. He had wandered down towards a dry stone wall, leaving pawprints in the slope that I really didn't fancy following. I called him across and at first I thought perhaps my voice had got lost on the breeze.

'Come back!' I called out, louder this time. 'Hurry up, Harry!'

I had good sight of him and could see for myself that he wasn't responding. Instead, he started pacing up and down the length of the wall. Then, as it occurred to me that Harry might have found something, another dog jumped up from behind the wall as if trying in vain to get over. As soon as I caught sight of the spaniel and the blue harness it was wearing, I charged across the field.

'Monty!' I called out. 'Stay where you are, boy!'

In response, the lost spaniel raced away in the opposite direction. I came to a halt as he tore across a field thick with reeds and tuffets, heading towards the southern shore of the lake. Monty was quite clearly frightened and I figured that a stranger charging after him wasn't going to help. So, as Paddy and Max joined me, while Harry held station at the wall, I took out my phone and called the number I had noted from the appeal.

'The good news is that Monty's alive and well!' I told the owner, a lovely local lady named Alison, and explained where I had seen him. 'The bad news is that he's bolted, but if you can head towards the top of the lake, you stand a good chance of finding him there. He's very unlikely to stray any other way unless he's into mountaineering. I'll stay here with my dogs. If he doubles back, we'll be ready.'

With Harry back on the path where it was drier, we stood on watch for the next half an hour. All three dogs were quite content to sniff about, but I kept a close eye on Harry – if Monty tried to slip south, I figured he would know about it. When my phone rang, I pressed it to my ear immediately.

'We've got him!' said Alison, who sounded close to tears of happiness. 'Thank you so much!'

'Don't thank me,' I said, with one eye on Harry.

A few days later, shortly before Christmas, I invited Alison and Monty to join us for a livestream walk. With Monty on a lead, securely reunited with his owner, we walked and talked about the drama. After the appeal had been posted on Max's Facebook page, people had been messaging in from all around the world to share concern and ask for updates. A livestream seemed like the most effective way to share the happy ending and confirm that Monty was safe and unharmed by his ordeal. It was just one of those lovely feelgood stories to mark the Christmas season. In the days that followed, it even crept into the national news. Ultimately, it was a chance for Harry the Spaniel Finder General to enjoy some well-earned praise.

Harry is a unique character. He's always been very different from Paddy, just as Max was one of a kind. Together, their different ages also defined them and I loved how they supported one another as the Brown-Legged Gang. As a collective their qualities combined to become a force greater than the sum of its parts. People loved seeing them together, either online in livestreams, in person at events or even just out and about in the Lake District. Every single day, I'd open emails and notes from individuals who wanted to express what an inspiration the dogs had been. Max, Paddy and Harry didn't possess superhero powers. As Springer Spaniels, they carried boundless energy, loyalty and love, and I had given them a platform to share it. They found joy in everything and I think that's what draws those who are finding life to be a challenge. The three dogs are a constant reminder to seize each day and make the most of it. They're an inspiration to us all and a catalyst for encouraging us to look after each other.

*   *   *

Looking back at that year, I feel there was one story more than any other that really brought home to me the healing power of dogs. Just before Harry's birthday, the parents of a young teenage girl reached out to me. Charlotte had been living with a chronic eating disorder for some time and had become seriously ill. She'd been hospitalised several times and her life was in danger. Her mother and father, as well as her younger sister, had shown her so much love and support, but ultimately Charlotte's recovery was in her hands. She recognised this for herself and wanted to get better.

As someone who had loved the outdoors, Charlotte always enjoyed visiting the Lake District; she was also an avid follower of Max's Facebook page. So, when her parents contacted me to share her story and asked if they could arrange for their daughter to meet the dogs, I was more than happy to oblige. I even invited them to join us on a walk to celebrate Harry's special day. We made it a surprise, which was so lovely even if it did take a bit of coordination!

The first step was for Charlotte's parents to persuade her to join them on a trip to Derwentwater. Knowing what time they'd arrive, I parked up in a layby on the road to the lake with the dogs. When the family appeared in my wing mirror and Charlotte's father covertly flashed his lights, I pulled out ahead of them. Charlotte recognised the van straight away and apparently responded with amazement when we stopped at the same destination. I opened up the doors to let the dogs out and it was really quite moving to see her radiate in their presence. Standing back with Charlotte's mother, I listened to her talk about the ordeal they'd all been through and felt nothing but admiration for them. When I had the chance to talk to Charlotte herself, looking on the brink of despair, I saw a former version of myself before Max showed me the way.

'Please don't give up,' I told her. 'I nearly did, but then I saw the bigger picture. Just look around you. Look at the sky, the mountains and the lake. Nature is beautiful and so are your family and both will always be there to bring out the best in you.'

In among the tears and smiles, I hoped that she had heard me. I also knew that it wasn't me who could really connect with Charlotte, it was the dogs who seemed to bring so much light into her eyes as we walked. I saw nothing but happiness in their time together and it was an honour when Charlotte and her wonderful family later accepted my invitation to come along to Memory Wood and plant a tree.

Shortly afterwards, Charlotte wrote to me. For someone so young, she had such an incisive and beautiful way with words and what she had to share tugged at my heart:

> **Meeting Max, Paddy and Harry was the start**
> **of my recovery. They helped to bring**
> **the real me back, the real Charlotte,**
> **and for that I am eternally grateful.**

That letter meant so much to me and I read it through misting eyes. What's more, I discovered that her little sister had also added a note of thanks. Reading between the lines, it's easy to forget that friends and family of people who struggle with personal issues can also be deeply affected. The road to recovery is never easy for anyone, but if there's one thing I've learned from personal experience, it's the fact that dogs can show us the way. And if you happen to be lost or feeling trapped, maybe someone like Harry can help.

18
Say Hello

PADDY'S FIFTH BIRTHDAY CAME AT PRECISELY the right time. In January 2022, after a long winter of concern for Max, we had the chance to raise almost £30,000 for GNAAS in celebration of Cumbria's coolest Springer Spaniel. Paddy had the time of his life, as he does every day, and we finished with a splash in the lake from his favourite shore. In the same month, he and Bella rekindled their special relationship, which meant we could look forward to a second litter of pups in the spring. At a time when my focus was on caring for an ageing dog, it was such a joy to be reminded that both Paddy and Harry still had so much of their lives ahead of them.

Both dogs were so good with Max. As he slowed down, they were kind and patient with him. For a dog that liked to move at about 100 miles an hour, Paddy put the brakes on around Max. He never complained when we kept our walks short, knowing that I would make it up to him later when Max was snoozing. Paddy,

Harry and I would often slip out so they could get the runaround they needed. On our return, Harry always bounded up to Max. They were so pleased to see each other. I like to think that Harry was enthusiastically recounting the high points of our walk so that Max didn't feel as if he had missed out.

Max's frailty constantly reminded me that his better days were long gone and yet there was a simple pleasure to be had from just a short walk together. He also still saw a great deal of his friends. Angela and I would often be joined by Lisa, Adam, Bella and Mabel, as well as Amanda, Rob, Archie and Furgus. Often, someone would take the younger dogs off for a roam, leaving Max and me with whoever chose to keep us company.

We had a favourite walk along the lane beside Thirlmere reservoir. It was quiet, sheltered, secluded and overlooked the water. Crucially, it was also flat, which made it easier for Max. With banked woodland for the other dogs to explore, it offered something for everybody. When Max was ready to turn around, we could head back to the van. There, he could settle in his basket with the side door open until everyone else came back. On one such return journey, Max had dropped back to walk beside Angela and one of our friends. I was just ahead with Paddy, throwing a tennis ball for him, when she screamed: *'Kerry! Max has collapsed!'*

As soon as I spun around, I knew it was another vestibular attack. Max was on the ground once again, struggling to get onto his feet. Rushing back, I scooped him into my arms and carried him the short distance back to the van.

'He'll be OK,' I assured Angela. It was the first time she had seen him suffer an episode and I had been just as shocked when he first collapsed on the front path. 'Won't you, buddy?' I added under my breath, almost pleading with Max because I suddenly felt quite helpless.

Within minutes, following a phone call, Amanda arrived back with the group that had gone ahead. I had managed to calm Max, who was lying in his basket in the back of the van.

'If today is the day he goes,' I said shakily as she examined him and paused to hold back tears, 'then he's with his friends and he's enjoyed a nice walk.'

With great care, and with the calm manner of a brilliant vet, Amanda lifted Max out of the van and encouraged him to walk towards her. He was a little unsteady, but with his tail wagging, he took a few steps forward. Already he was looking brighter.

'It's not time yet,' she said to reassure me and helped Max back into his basket. 'Give him a few hours to rest and he'll recover. The effects are passing and he's still happy.'

*　　*　　*

At teatime that evening, Max finished his supper as usual and then cleaned up the kibbles left behind by

Paddy and Harry. He seemed absolutely fine, just as Amanda had said. It had been an unsettling episode, however, and one I had been braced for since his first collapse. I also knew that it wouldn't be the last and again I started to torment myself about what was right for Max. He *seemed* content, if increasingly tired, but was it right to let him continue experiencing such distressing vestibular episodes? It was a question that kept me awake at night throughout the nights that followed.

One day that week, a moment of light shone through the gloom. It arrived in the form of a call from Lisa and Adam to say that Bella's litter was on its way. The vet had estimated that she was carrying seven puppies. This time, nobody expected that number. There would be three huge pups, I predicted. And I was delighted to be proven wrong.

Having rushed over by invitation that evening, I even fired up the livestream so that Max's online community could share in the delightful sight of *seven* precious pups. It's just so magical to watch them come into this world and then make their way to the milk bar. Every time it brings me to tears and on this occasion I was already feeling emotional. I was so happy for Bella and Paddy, knowing their pups would all be going to loving homes, yet my thoughts remained with Max. As delightful as it was to see the newborns, I knew that he would never see them for himself.

The third attack was a bad one. We had been out with Paddy and Harry, just over a week after his second episode, and I'd had to deal with it alone. As I couldn't get Max to stand, I carried him to the van and we headed straight for our vet's surgery. This time, out of hours on a Sunday, we were seen by a locum. As a stand-in vet, she didn't know Max and it felt like she wasn't listening to me as she read through his notes.

'Last time he had some anti-sickness pills,' I said. 'They helped.'

The vet switched from her computer screen to peer into Max's eyes once more, which were still flicking from side to side.

'He has a brain tumour,' she announced abruptly. 'I don't think Max has long left so you might want to think about putting him down.'

'Sorry, what?' I just couldn't process what she'd said.

'We can do it now if you wish?'

Now, I know she had a difficult job to do, but what the vet proposed seemed both brutal and unthinkable. After a lifetime together, there was no way I could let Max go just like that.

'I'm grateful to you for seeing us,' I said, 'but even if it is his time, it won't end here.'

On the drive to the house, reality hit home. I had persuaded the vet to at least give Max the same shot as last time. It meant he was calm and resting in his basket in the back of the van, while I sat behind the wheel, feeling tearful and angry. I knew full well that the vet was only doing her job, and very well at that. She might have been abrupt in making her diagnosis, but I recognised that a tumour was the most likely cause of the attacks – I just hadn't responded well when she had spelled it out. Even so, this wasn't about the care Max received but the bond I shared with him. Since we found each other, he had been at my side throughout. We had cared for each other, but now our journey through that shared life was reaching an end. I had done everything I could do to make sure he was safe, healthy and happy. I didn't want him to suffer, nor did I wish to keep him alive just to spare myself from grief. It would have been the easier decision, but also deeply selfish.

Whatever was causing Max's vestibular attacks, my main concern was the fact that they were intensifying. If each episode was distressing for me, I couldn't imagine how it must be for him. On that journey over the fells, as I processed the situation I recognised that we were in a different place now. My sweet old boy was reaching the end and I had a responsibility to oversee that in a way that honoured exactly how much he meant to me. In my mind, I knew it was time. Outwardly, I pulled up outside our house in tears.

'Oh, Max,' I said, on helping him up the path as Paddy and Harry escorted us to the door. 'We'll make it right, I promise.'

*   *   *

The next morning, I called Amanda to update her. In her role as a vet as much as a friend, she came out to meet me and examine Max. As I stood back so that she could work, listening to her speak so kindly to him, I felt so much better about the situation: we were in good care and that meant so much to me at this difficult time.

'Kerry,' she said afterwards, 'what would you like to do?'

Amanda had reiterated that without a scan, the diagnosis of a brain tumour remained a probability. It was also clear to me that even with that knowledge there was little that could be done, given Max's age. I knew it was time to say goodbye, I just wanted to do it in the best way possible that put his welfare first and I knew she could help.

'For whatever time he has left,' I said, 'can I register Max with you as a vet?'

'Of course,' she said. 'Consider it done.'

'And you'll let me know?' I added. 'When it's time?'

It was the one thing that continued to trouble me. I was so torn. In my head, I accepted that Max was in the final stage of his life. I was absolutely clear with myself that I didn't want him to suffer in any way. In my heart, of course, I couldn't bear to let him go.

'I promised you that I would do that,' Amanda said to reassure me. 'Nothing has changed. Right now, Max is comfortable and content just being with you. It's the only thing that should matter to you now.'

I knew that I could count on Amanda and that came as such a relief. It helped me to think about how Max would want to go. I was also very aware that he hadn't touched only my life. An entire community had grown around him. He meant so much to people in different ways and I felt I had a duty to prepare them. Part of me wanted to hide the situation, but I knew that would make things worse in the long run. We shared our walks with the community every day – I had to let them know that one day soon Max would no longer be with us.

And so I penned an update, which broke my heart. Having decided to be completely transparent about the situation, I explained about Max's vestibular attacks and the prognosis in view of his advanced age. Once I'd published the post, I set my phone to one side and spent time with my dogs. I took them up to The Paw Store, where they settled on the sofa as usual. That sense of normality was so important to me and I hoped it would be the same for Max, Paddy and Harry.

Later that day, when I picked up my phone to see how people had responded to my update, I had to stop scroll-ing through the sea of orange hearts and just bowed my head in grief.

'Max,' I said, 'you really are the world's most-loved dog.'

*   *   *

Amanda visited Max the next day and the day after that. He was still a little wobbly on standing and though clearly weak, his spirit was intact – I could still catch his eye and know that he registered me in the same way as he always had. I came to relish these small moments and yet I knew not to cling to them in false hope. Instead, with messages still pouring in from Max's online community, I took comfort in the fact that I wasn't facing this moment alone.

A few weeks earlier, the dogs and I had been invited to help celebrate the opening of a refurbished local inn. It was a popular spot with a welcoming atmosphere and glorious lakeside view. I had always intended to bring Paddy and Harry as we planned to mark the opening with a sponsored walk in aid of GNAAS, while leaving Max at home with Angela. Ever since the unveiling of the statue, I had pulled him back from the public eye. With precious time remaining, however, and the opening of the inn scheduled for the weekend, I wondered whether Max might enjoy taking part in the event in a limited way. As I saw things, it would be an opportunity for him to do something he had always loved, which was to be around people.

So, following a call to the organiser to confirm that we would still be there, I followed up the sad news that I had shared on Facebook with a post to say that Max would in fact be present for the start and finish of the walk. Angela had kindly offered to join us and stay with him by the fireside while anyone who wished to enjoy some fresh air could accompany Paddy, Harry and me. *Please do come and say hello,* I had written, even though we all knew it was really a chance to say goodbye.

The invitation would prove to be one that wasn't ignored. As soon as we arrived ahead of the event, one glimpse at the huge number of people gathering outside the inn told me this would be a memorable day.

'Thank you for coming with us,' I told Angela. 'I wouldn't want to leave Max with anyone else.'

'We'll be fine,' she said gently as I spotted Amanda and her family along with many other familiar, friendly faces. 'Max and I are looking forward to staying warm and toasty by the fire.'

* * *

For all the smiles as we set off on our hike, having celebrated the reopening of a fantastic inn, I couldn't stop thinking about Max. I was so used to his presence at my side. I realised this would be my first group walk without him and despite the numbers around me, I felt quite alone. Leaving him made me feel so anxious and in the first few minutes I thought about making my excuses and heading back to join him. I knew that I could count on Paddy and Harry to get me round, however. They were so full of positivity and life, as were all the other dogs who joined us. I was also in good company – so many people on that hike were aware of what I was going through.

Slowly, as we walked and talked, I was feeling much better. As we reached the midway point, I found myself chatting to a very pleasant lady with a spaniel of her own. We were exchanging stories about how lively they can be when she revealed something that stopped me in my tracks.

'I just want to say thanks to you, Max, Paddy and Harry for saving my life,' she said. 'I was in a dark place and it was only by seeing what spaniels had done for you that I decided to get one for myself.' She paused there to consider the dog trotting happily beside her. 'Can I give you a hug?' she asked and before I could respond, she'd wrapped her arms around me.

It was a moment that took me by complete surprise, but also meant so much to me. It was such a brave thing for her to say and do, and I was delighted that her dog had given her purpose in life.

As we ambled our way back to the inn, yet more people approached me with their stories. I was so moved to hear them all. By the time we returned to the inn for lunch, I was really glad that I hadn't backed out of that walk. It had lifted my spirits no end and then seeing Max once more just brought my sun out from behind the clouds.

Throughout lunch, as people got to know each other and bonded over a love of dogs and countryside walks,

Max sat under my chair with his head on his paws and slept. I liked to think that he was absorbing it all in his own way. Sometimes he'd stir, but his chin never left the ground. As always, it felt like he was at the heart of so much joy and generosity of spirit and we went home that afternoon having raised over £2,000 for GNAAS. It felt like the end to a worthwhile day, not just for the charity but also as a way for Max to take a final bow before members of a community that had formed around him. Emotionally as well as physically, it had been a tiring day, and so when the phone rang that evening, I took a breath in surprise.

'I was watching Max over lunch ...' said Amanda.

I knew what would follow as she paused for a moment. For she hadn't been alone in seeing it in those moments when he opened his tired eyes from under the table. I had seen it, too. He'd also remained quite still on my lap when the phone startled me. He'd had enough. For all the love that surrounded my dear old dog, Max didn't want to be here any longer.

'Kerry, it's time.'

19

One Last Walk

OVER THE PHONE, STRUGGLING TO SPEAK with a catch in my throat, I had arranged with Amanda to check in with her the next day and settle upon a time and place. On that Sunday night, having talked it through with Angela, I had midweek in mind. That would give me a couple of days to prepare and say goodbye to Max in a way that felt fitting for us both.

All I knew was that I didn't want Max to go to sleep on a veterinary table. It just didn't seem right and so it came as a huge relief when Amanda said that she understood and agreed to my timeframe. It meant I had a short time to settle on an appropriate location for the final farewell. In my mind, it had to be a favourite place for Max. Somewhere outdoors that I knew he loved. That night, I went to bed reliving practically every walk we had ever enjoyed across the Lake District. It made me realise just how many miles we'd covered together and how many memories I had to treasure forever.

The next morning, in the light of a new day, my conversation with Amanda seemed slightly unreal. When she called me as planned, I even wondered whether we should review our decision.

'When Max woke this morning, he wagged his tail,' I said hopefully. 'That must be a sign that he's happy?'

'His tail will always wag when you're there,' said Amanda in a way that made me feel this wasn't the first time someone in my position had sought reasons to delay the inevitable. 'Putting a dog to sleep is one of the hardest things an owner must decide to do,' she continued. 'Now you could wait, but he's likely to have another vestibular attack. Having been through so much, he may not survive it.'

'Which would be unthinkable,' I said.

'In my experience,' Amanda said after a moment, 'nobody ever regrets going too early, but they do when it's too late.'

I nodded to myself before responding.

'I've thought of a place,' I told her. 'In fact, all the dogs enjoy it there.'

'I know where you have in mind,' Amanda replied. 'It's always your first suggestion whenever we all go for a walk. We all love it, in fact.'

It was a moment of lightness that I needed. I was also very glad that I wasn't alone in considering this place to be special.

'Can I have one more day with Max?' I asked and closed my eyes to hold back the tears when Amanda encouraged me to treasure it.

*   *   *

This would be the best day ever. That was how I approached it, even though it broke my heart into pieces. I couldn't bring myself to think of it as a final one with Max – it was too much for me. So, instead, I set out to give him the most joyful experience from first light until nightfall. Without thinking ahead, I just wanted us both to live in each moment.

'Here you are, Max. This is going to be a surprise ...'

It started with breakfast. Normally, I measured out the dried food for Max, Paddy and Harry to keep them fit and healthy. Max always managed to find a little more by cleaning up after his messier dining companions. On this occasion, however, there was no need – I filled his bowl with as much as he could manage and set it before him.

'I know, right?' I smiled to myself as Max tucked in. 'Happy days!'

From there, having slept off his huge start to the day, I took the dogs on a tour of all our regular walks. We set off in the van and stopped at places Max recognised. From hill-tops to woodland trails – and the path leading up to Memory Wood – we'd hop out so he could sniff

and toddle around before moving on to our next destination. Even though we didn't walk far, it proved to be
quite a tiring exercise and so afterwards we stopped at
The Paw Store for an afternoon nap. People regularly
send the dogs lovely treats in the post. I kept them on a
high shelf, but they'd learned to become suddenly alert
whenever I moved towards it.

'What would you like, Max?' I asked this time. 'How
about a chew? Salmon, beef or both?'

Without turning to look at him, I already knew the
answer. I also made sure that Paddy and Harry weren't
left out. The chews proved quite resilient in their jaws
and so I just sat back to watch three Springer Spaniels
do their very best to demolish them. I found myself
gazing at Max, of course, and treasured this small escape
from reality. Of course I knew that time was running
out, an ache already forming in my chest, but we'd made
the most of every second.

*   *   *

Back home, as the day drew to a close, I couldn't help
but feel sombre. The dogs had flopped into their baskets,
nodding off to the patter of rain outside, but the stillness
that settled in with them seemed more intense than
usual. Angela and I sat together for some time and
talked about the memorable moments we'd shared with
Max. We both knew that I owed him my life. Without
him, I might not have been here at all. Over the years,

Max had left his pawprints across our lives, as well as Angela's hallway, but I tried to mop those up before she noticed. Even when she did, Max could be easily forgiven. His friendship with her late father, Alistair, had been very special and Max had been there for her after he passed. Over time, in fact, Angela had grown incredibly close to him in her own way. She was never going to be entirely comfortable with dog hair on the sofa, but that evening I knew she loved him very much.

'This is unbearable,' she said at one point after we had fallen into a reflective silence. 'We could just call Amanda right now and put Max to sleep ...'

Angela took a breath only for tears to take over, but what she was about to say had been on my mind as well. We were in a situation no dog owner wants to experience. Having made the decision, however – and I knew it was the right one for Max – I felt we just had to live with the inevitable feeling of guilt and doubt that weighed heavily on us both.

'There's not long now,' I said to console her. 'Let's do this in the best way that we can.'

*　　*　　*

After another big breakfast the next morning, there was one last place that I wanted to visit with Max. It was also only a short walk from home. We took our time, however, and both Paddy and Harry walked at our pace. I was aware that I hadn't given them the same attention recently as I had to Max. I also sensed that they understood why, just as they knew where we were heading.

'Here we are,' I said as we reached the entrance to the churchyard. 'Back to where it all started.'

When Max and I first met and I had sought permission from his former owner to take him up here for some exercise, the churchyard bench overlooking Keswick formed the boundary of my world. It was the furthest I had ventured from the house in years. Arriving there with Max had felt like a liberation and for some time it became a regular place for us to visit. We'd sit there together, listening to the hum of the market town far below, enjoying the view that stretched across the lake to the fells beyond.

Back in those days, Max used to make a beeline for a rabbit warren behind an old gravestone. If any rabbits were on the surface when he bounded across, they quickly outwitted him and vanished into the earth. As I headed for the bench, he broke away for one last look. It reminded me of an old soldier revisiting a scene of battle, where once sworn foes had grown to respect each other over time.

As Paddy and Harry explored the grounds, Max came to join me on the bench. Bless him, he was so tired and I helped him up so he could sit beside me. For a moment, we just gazed out at a landscape that had once seemed off limits to us both. Everywhere I looked told a story about our lives together. Then I found Hope Park and realised I could just about see that statue of a much beloved dog on a bench.

'That's you,' I said, with my arm around him. 'You'll always be there.'

I hadn't come here just to reflect, it also felt like a fitting place to stage our regular livestream. I still wanted to be honest with people – they had formed a bond with Max as much as I had and I felt like I owed them this moment. There would be no walk today, I explained as the viewing count started to climb, and went on to explain as sensitively as I could that we had entered Max's last hours. It was a deeply emotional broadcast and having thanked everyone for showing him such love and loyalty, I stopped before my voice cracked apart. And as I did so, with dear Max at my side, the church bells from the top of the tower behind me rang out far and wide.

*   *   *

Later that morning, we paid a last visit to Derwentwater. Naturally, Paddy and Harry bounded in and within seconds were swimming for sticks. Max had left all that behind some time ago. He was happy standing in the shallows, watching them at play. Compared to the day before, I was finding this increasingly tough. Every emotion that I experienced felt intense, from love and longing to a sense of awful guilt that would not leave me despite knowing we were doing the kindest thing for him. When I called him out of the water, he showed no sign of reluctance. As a younger dog, he could be a rascal and simply head further out. This time, he just looked at me as if to say all he really wanted right now was a rest.

'Let's go home,' I said and summoned Paddy and Harry to the shore. 'It'll come, Max. There's just one last person we need to see.'

Normally at that time I would have had lunch. I tried to eat but found I wasn't hungry. I had prepared something for Angela, but it was more of a token because I felt sure she'd also have no appetite. So, I just sat opposite her place at the kitchen table and waited with Paddy and Harry for company.

From upstairs, all I could hear was weeping. It tore me apart to hear, but I knew it was an important moment. After we'd returned home, I'd suggested to Angela that if she wanted to say anything to Max then now would be the right time. She'd already told me that she couldn't face being present when the time came and I completely respected her for that so I had given her space to say what she needed to say to him and then headed downstairs. As I sat there, listening to my wife weeping, I found both Paddy and Harry nuzzling my hands.

'Boys, this is the saddest moment of my life. I need you both now more than ever.'

Paddy licked the back of my hand in response. Harry looked at me with that gentle gaze I always found so calming. It was enough to persuade me to let Angela know that we were here for her whenever she needed us. So, I crept upstairs to signal that she wasn't alone. As I climbed the steps, aware that I would soon be leaving the house with Max for the last time, I found her hugging him on the floor with her head buried in his coat. Max just lay there and though I couldn't see his face, that wagging tail spoke volumes.

*   *   *

Manesty Woods. After such a wonderful life, it had to be where Max came to rest. Before setting off on that solemn journey, I had checked in with Amanda to let her know we were on our way. She had been so kind in agreeing to put Max to sleep at a location of our choosing and set off with her veterinary bag and an assistant from her practice. It was only a short drive around Derwentwater. No more than fifteen minutes or so around the lakeside road, but in that time, I knew we were doing the right thing. With Paddy and Harry in the back of the van, Max travelled beside me. He looked absolutely exhausted, curled up on the passenger seat, as if perhaps this final hour was all that he could manage.

'We'll soon be there,' I told him and in my mind I saw this destination as a gateway for him to embark upon another grand adventure. It would be without me this time, but I knew a dog who had shown such unswerving loyalty would never truly leave us. 'You'll soon be on your way, Max.'

It had been raining on and off all day. We were lucky on our visit to the churchyard, but drizzle was falling when we dropped by the lake. Lunch had seen a brief downpour, but now that low front seemed to be passing. The veils of thick mist that had clung to the peaks slowly drifted away and as the clouds began to pull apart, it felt as if the stage was set. The air felt fresh and the ground seemed cleansed somehow. It was only when we pulled off the lane at the entrance to the woods that I realised Amanda had brought her dogs with her. She had parked her car just up the track, close to the glade where I would share my final moments with Max. Over the phone, my veterinary friend had stressed that I should take my time to say goodbye. When I was ready, she and her assistant would quietly join us and put Max to sleep with the care and compassion that was so important to me. Just then, however, Paddy and Harry spotted Archie and Furgus. Before I'd even switched off the engine, they were straining to jump out so they could play. It all felt very natural, which is just how I wanted it to be.

'What do you say to one last walk?' I asked Max, having first opened the side door so the other two could tear off to join Amanda's dogs. 'We'll go no further than our first steps together.'

With some effort he lifted his head and those dark hazel eyes met my gaze as they had so many times throughout the years. Despite everything, Max was still there for me. Loyal to the end, as I was to him. With great care, I placed him on the ground so he could walk at my side. As I did so, sunshine swept over the woods and glittered across the water. Then, as the other dogs came alive in a setting that they loved so passionately, I accompanied my very best friend to a place where he could come to rest at last and leave us in love and light.

Part Four

20

Biscuits and Sunbeams

WHEN WE LOSE A LOVED ONE, their absence is felt everywhere. It's as if a veil of emptiness has fallen across the world, settling on everything. Before dawn the next morning, I set off for the first walk of the day with only Paddy and Harry. That was unusual in itself and the fact that we moved at a quicker pace than we had in recent months reminded me what was missing. With every step, I couldn't stop thinking about him: Max was gone.

Before Manesty, I had worried about how I'd cope. Losing Max had been unthinkable for so long and yet on our return home I felt strangely at peace. Why? Because we had done it right. I realised I was fortunate in being friends with a vet who allowed us to say farewell to him in the most beautiful way, but long before that we had made the most of our lives together. Ever since we found each other, Max and I had seized every day. Now that had come to an end, but I found that I could look back with no regrets. If anything, I realised that I had put myself under a huge amount of stress about doing everything properly for him as the time approached. Now that I could tell myself that we had done just that, it felt like a weight had lifted. Above all, I could take comfort in the fact that Max had made this world a better place. He had brought hope, courage and positivity to so many and proved a faithful companion not just to me but also Paddy and Harry.

Shortly before he closed his eyes for the final time, I had called them both to join us. I didn't want them to find that Max had just gone and so they were present as Amanda carried out her work. She did so with such care and sensitivity, and a sense of calm prevailed as Max slipped away. Afterwards, as he lay quite still in my arms, Paddy and then Harry checked over him as dogs do before leaving us to talk about the milestones in his life. Even before I'd returned home, I knew that we had done the very best for Max throughout the final chapter of his life and that helped to soften the pain.

Back home, after our quiet, reflective walk on that morning afterwards, I followed our usual routine. Paddy and Harry padded through the hallway and into the kitchen before looking at me expectantly. This was something they did every morning, as if perhaps fearing that one day I might completely forget about breakfast.

'It's next on my list,' I assured them and felt strangely comforted at the prospect of checking off everyday tasks. As I measured out the dogs' feed, I was already thinking about the orders I needed to process at The

Paw Store. In recent days I had fallen behind somewhat, for understandable reasons, but now I was looking forward to being busy again. 'Here you go, boys. Tuck in!'

I was aware of Max's bowl. It sat empty on the floor beside the other two, but that was OK. Ever since the drive back from Manesty, his belongings seemed to hold new meaning. From the blankets he slept on, which smelled just like him, to the brush with hairs from his coat snagged in the bristles, it all reminded me that he had gone. I also accepted that it was part of the grieving process and something I'd come to accept over time. I had no plans to clear his things away. All three dogs used to mix and match when it came to leads and baskets, and I wanted to keep things normal for Paddy and Harry. What's more, I found I liked having these things around me. I'd kept his orange collar, of course, and that remained on the sideboard, where I had placed it the day before. As the two dogs piled into their break-fast, I picked it up and ran my thumb over his identity tag. It was speckled in mud and I wanted to restore the shine. As I did so, Paddy switched his attention to the water bowl and Harry made himself comfortable by the back door. I glanced down at their bowls, just to check they'd finished eating.

Noting the scattering of kibble that they had left behind on the floor, I gestured for Max to tidy up after them. It was all part of our breakfast routine and he was always so good at waiting for me to give him the green light. Catching myself instinctively directing him towards his little reward, I gasped as if I'd momentarily forgotten to breathe. I looked at Paddy and Harry, blinking back to reality, before falling into a kitchen chair and sobbing into my hands.

This couldn't be an ordinary day. Max was no longer here and that reshaped every moment.

*   *   *

I had no plans to livestream a walk that morning. I had posted a note on Max's Facebook page to say that he had passed away, but hadn't read the flood of messages that followed because I just didn't feel ready. I needed time and space, I had thought to myself, as Paddy, Harry and I set out along a track still damp from the recent rain. But within a mile, I was walking with my phone in hand and the camera trained on the dogs as they roamed ahead of me.

'So, we've lost him,' I said, having decided to broadcast because that moment felt like something I needed to share. 'Max has gone.'

I barely got through a minute before my emotions got the better of me. It was the sense of connection with his online community that broke me for as the viewing numbers climbed so a stream of hearts floated up the screen. I had always known that Max's death would have an impact that went far wider than my household and as soon as I reached out to the people who loved him in their own way, I felt their grief as much as my own.

I didn't broadcast for long, but I'm glad that I had at least made that connection. Looking back, had I chosen to close myself away with Paddy and Harry, I might never have gone live on a walk again. As we wandered on, I felt like it had been in keeping with the spirit of Max for he had encouraged me, as much as everyone who knew him, to reach out and draw strength from each other. I was heartbroken, of course, and now the tears had started they fell frequently, but I also knew that I would get through this – I had Paddy and Harry, after all. As we neared the end of our walk, I was mindful of the landscape in the air created by banks of huge, sculpted clouds. As shapes formed and then drifted apart, high up in the sky, I saw it as a world above our own and that helped me to feel as if Max was watching over us.

Grief can affect us in all sorts of different ways. Even those seasoned to loss can be surprised at how it affects them. I felt I had been prepared for Max to go. I had given some thought to how I would feel afterwards and yet within the space of a day I was in uncharted territory. Although I had hoped some time in The Paw Store would help, once I started work, I found that I couldn't focus. I was processing orders and catching up on emails, but my thoughts were elsewhere. It didn't feel right to be so disengaged with work I loved and so I took the dogs back home. It was good to see Angela and though she too had tried to keep busy, we found ourselves just sitting and sharing our favourite stories about Max. It was nice and we shared laughs as well as tears.

Later, as Paddy and Harry began to pace and grow restless, I suggested that we take them out to stretch our legs.

'Where shall we go?' asked Angela.

'I was thinking Walla Crag.'

As soon as I suggested it, I could see Angela processing what that would mean. The path up to the fell in question can be steep in places. As a result, we hadn't ventured up there for some time as it would have been too much for Max, though he'd loved it as a younger dog. The views over Derwentwater from such a lofty plateau are magnificent and bring with them a real sense of peace and tranquility. Being up high above the world seemed like just the place to be. I could see from Angela's expression that she felt the same way.

'That would be perfect,' she said with a smile.

The clouds had thickened through the day. As we hiked our way up the path, it looked like the sunset I had been hoping to see from the summit would be hidden. I didn't mind – the fact that we were here, on a walk Max adored in his younger days, was enough for me. Once again, we were moving faster and further than we had done for the best part of a year. Paddy and Harry seemed glad to be out, while Angela and I picked our way along without a concern for anyone else but ourselves. I missed Max hugely, of course, but this was a new chapter for us all.

When it comes to hiking up fells, I always find it takes longer than planned. By the time we picked our way to the summit, the low cloud threatened rain again. It was a shame because we had come up here to admire the view and yet the light left the landscape somewhat subdued. Still, the dogs were having a great time and it really did feel good to be on a proper adventure again. Despite the possibility of drizzle, which we could see fall in pockets across the mountains, we stayed up there for some time. The breeze was light and even refreshing, while the natural landscape that spread far and wide seemed like the ideal stage for contemplation. Indeed, when my phone rang, it took me a moment to register.

'I have Max's ashes,' said Amanda after she had introduced herself and asked if this was a good time. Angela was taking photos of the dogs at play and so I turned away from them just to get out of the breeze. 'The crematorium thought you'd like them to come home as soon as possible.'

From the moment Max went to sleep, I hadn't really registered the formalities that followed. All I knew was that Amanda had shown infinite kindness in taking his body away to prepare for this moment. She had made all the arrangements with the crematorium, who told her they were familiar with Max. It was so nice to hear that as I could feel assured that he had been handled with care and respect.

'I don't know how to begin thanking you,' I said. 'If we could have him home for one night, that would mean so much.'

'Have you decided what you might do with them?' she asked.

It had been a question I'd considered so many times in recent days. I just hadn't settled on an answer. All I knew was that Max belonged outdoors in a world that he had made his own. Then I considered all the places that he loved across the Lake District and simply felt overwhelmed.

'I've been giving it some thought,' I told Amanda and as I drew breath to say that I needed more time, my attention turned to the skies. For in that moment the late sun had broken through the cloud. Given the hour, the light from the southwest was a fiery orange. Immediately, I was reminded of Max's collar. As the low beams slanted across the landscape, my gaze was drawn in the direction of Memory Wood. With my phone still pressed to my ear, and our veterinary friend on the other end of the line, I nodded to myself. 'And I know just where he needs to be,' I added.

21
Powered by Max

THE FOLLOWING WEEKEND, to the sound of skylarks from the upper fell, Angela and I gathered with a small group of friends of Max and prepared to lay him to rest. Some had brought their own dogs, which meant Paddy and Harry had plenty of company amid the sapling trees we had planted. Amanda and Rob were present, as were Adam and Lisa. A few days before I had chosen a spot and completed the spadework for the small wooden casket that contained his ashes. I thanked everyone for coming and recounted the last time Max had visited this place.

'It was a long way to come for an elderly dog, but he pulled me along the path as if he had something to show me ...' I paused for a moment, my head bowed. 'I like to think we're standing before that place because if there's one thing Max loved as much as me, it's a view.'

A patter of laughter helped me to feel that I had sounded the right tone. For I wanted this moment to be a celebration and not just for me but for the little girl I had invited to help me place the casket in the ground.

*   *   *

When she learned that Max had passed away, Sophie was inconsolable. Ever since she was seven years old, when Max became a port in a storm for her as she struggled at school, they had formed such a close bond. Five years later, when it came to introducing Bronze Max to the world, it had been a great privilege for me to invite Sophie to do the honours. Now, on this sad occasion, I had asked if she would be at my side because I hoped it would help to bring her closure.

'We can do this,' I said to her quietly as we prepared to lay Max to rest. 'Together.'

Earlier that week, Sophie and her mum, Nicola, had visited The Paw Store. Straight away, I could tell that Sophie had been struggling with news of Max's passing. She was subdued and the rims under her eyes told me she had been crying. Paddy and Harry sat with her and she stroked their ears as I made a brew for Nicola.

'If she has any questions then she only has to ask,' I said to Nicola. 'Whatever it takes to help Sophie make sense of the situation, we're here for you both.'

I remembered vividly how tough it can be to process raw emotions at such a young age. I had grown up with a challenging stepfather and everything from sadness to rage could seem overwhelming to me back then. Dealing with death is an inevitability of life and never easy at any age, but I sensed that Sophie was finding it tougher than those with experience behind them.

'Well, she does have one question,' said Nicola, keeping her voice low. 'She's worried that Max never knew how much she loved him.'

I blinked hard as I handed Nicola her tea.

'Sophie,' I said next, and cleared my throat, 'I was wondering whether you'd like to write a letter to Max? You can seal it in an envelope and place it in his casket. That way, nobody else will read it but him.'

Sophie looked to her mother, who smiled and told her that was a lovely idea.

And so it was that having carefully lowered Max's casket into the ground with Sophie, I invited her to tuck her note in beside it. She had written it all by herself at home, taking her time to say everything she needed to say, and then written his name on the front.

'There,' I said and winked at her. 'That will mean the world to Max.'

From there, everyone present took turns to throw a little handful of soil on top. Some said a few words, others cried, and by the time we were done the ground was covered once again. I had brought a packet of wild-flower seeds with me, which we scattered to close this informal ceremony. Then, having carried some baskets and flasks with us, we sat down to enjoy a cup of tea and some cake. The sun came out as we chatted and laughter soon came to join the sound of the skylarks. It was lovely, and just as it should be.

*   *   *

As well as Max's immediate friends, his passing affected the wider community. I was overwhelmed by the kindness of people in the notes and cards they sent me. Max meant a great deal to so many and it was only natural that they would want to mark the loss in their own way. The good people of Hope Park staged a memorial walk, just days after we had laid Max to rest, and it was beautiful. This was swiftly followed by 'Paddy's Buttermere Bounce', which saw hundreds of people join us for another walk around the lake. What might have been a morose affair turned out to be a healing experience for us all. We talked about Max, of course, but also made the most of some lovely spring weather in good company to remind ourselves that life must go on. Indeed, over the weeks and months that followed, I found that life without Max became bearable. Slowly, his absence from every routine moment seemed to retreat from my thoughts. I would always miss him, but the pain of that loss began to ease. Paddy and Harry were central to the healing process. Their loyalty, energy and positivity set an example that I sought to follow. Max was gone but I had been so blessed to have him in my life and that came as a source of strength.

Ultimately, I knew that I would be all right. As time passed, I just wanted to be sure that little Sophie could also move on, feeling stronger for the experience. Her bond with Max had been extraordinary and the fact that she had written him a letter touched my heart. With this in mind, I decided to do something for her that I knew would have Max's blessing. With everything in place, I called her mum and invited them over to The Paw Store.

'Come in,' I said as Paddy and Harry fleeced Sophie for treats. 'We've all been looking forward to seeing you.'

In the time that she had known Max, Sophie had developed a passion for riding bicycles. She had progressed from peddling around her street to become serious as a mountain biker. Now she entered competitions and had really started to shine. I also knew that she was outgrowing her bike and so I asked her to take a look behind the wall of shelving by the door.

'Oh,' I heard her say, 'that's a nice bike.'

'Wheel it out so we can see,' I said. 'It's yours.'

I had already primed Nicola with what I had in mind – I just hadn't told her how closely tied it would be to the dog that meant so much to her daughter.

'It's orange!' Sophie looked both shocked and delighted at the brand-new mountain bike that gleamed under the spotlights. Paddy and Harry had crossed the floor to inspect it – they seemed to approve. 'My favourite.'

'Check out the frame,' I suggested.

Sophie crouched to find the vinyl wrapping I had added just for her and then read the wording out loud: 'Powered by Max.'

'Wherever you ride,' I told her, 'he'll be with you.'

I was so pleased that I'd had the chance to do this for her. Sophie really is a smashing young lady and Max brought out the best in her. After we'd finished with the thanks and tears, I asked her if she could do one small thing for me.

'Harry's collar is getting a little tatty,' I said. 'It's all the rabbit-hole inspections he likes to carry out.' Both she and her mother laughed. 'Would you mind swapping it for this one?'

I had placed Max's orange collar on the shelf beside me. Taking it in hand, having already replaced the identity tag, I offered it to Sophie. 'Harry was always looking out for Max in his old age. Now, Max can watch out for Harry.'

Without further word, I watched Sophie remove Harry's collar. He had always worn red ones since he was a puppy. Paddy would forever look good in green, but I felt that with this changing of the guard, it was only right that Harry should now carry Max's signature colour.

'It suits him,' she said and then wrapped her arms around him for the biggest hug that he had ever received.

'Well done, Harry,' I said as he looked at me. 'You've made a friend for life.'

*   *   *

Life would never be the same without Max. I knew that when it became apparent that his time with us was drawing to a close. But in the life that we shared together, he had taught me to look ahead with hope and positivity, be kind and find joy in moments we could easily take for granted. A walk in the fells, throwing balls for Paddy and Harry by the shore of the lake, planting saplings in Memory Wood, or just taking time to chat to people when they recognised my dogs, these small acts helped me to move on that year while keeping Max's spirit alive.

Sometimes, during quiet moments at the start or the end of the day, I would wander down to Hope Park. If nobody was around, I'd take a seat beside Max's statue. As Paddy and Harry swept the pathway for pigeons, I'd find myself talking to him in the same way that I always had and it was nice. In some ways it made me realise why so many people felt drawn to come here and I would leave feeling quite at peace with the world.

Ultimately, I knew that only time would help me come to terms with life after Max. That summer of 2022, together with Paddy and Harry, we rekindled our love of long walks and this included regular visits to Memory Wood. It was such a pleasure to see the wild flowers bloom for Max while the saplings spread their roots to grow taller and stronger. With bugs and birds in abundance, life was thriving here. The fact that it honoured those we had loved and lost made it all the more poignant to me.

Max would never be forgotten and as my life with Paddy and Harry regrouped without him, I was determined to build on his legacy. Uppermost on my mind was the amazing work carried out by the men and women of GNAAS. Ever since Paddy's birthday walk, and then Max's final appearance at the opening of the inn, I'd kept in close contact with the charity. As I learned about their work, the more my determination grew to support them. Everyone knew about the helicopters, of course. They're a visible reminder that we live in an isolated, mountainous environment. An early response to a medical emergency could mean the difference between life and death. Max had been a force for good when it came to raising funds for charity throughout his life and I intended to continue that work in his name.

In the summer, on what would have been Max's fifteenth birthday, Paddy, Harry and I staged a memorial walk called 'A Brew for Moo'. We invited people to join us for a leisurely ramble to Tewet Tarn, which offered an amazing view to the mighty slopes of Blencathra, followed by tea and cake. The response was overwhelming and the funds we raised for the charity continued to climb. Of course, it felt strange to be without Max, who had accompanied me from our very first walk, and yet as people arrived wearing orange shirts, badges and hats, I knew that he was with us. I was mindful of this as everyone gathered when their attention started turning to a point in the sky. At first, it was the sound that drew their attention, a rapid beating of blades, before the helicopter swooped over the ridge-line and then circled overhead.

'Is this for us?' someone asked me.

'It is indeed,' I said as the chopper came in to land. 'Say hello to the angels from GNAAS.'

As the event was raising money for their cause, it was amazing to see the paramedics jump out and then join us for a chat. I had been bowled over when I knew they would be coming and worked hard to keep it as a surprise. Naturally I trusted Paddy and Harry not to tell anyone – I just wasn't sure that I could say the same for myself! Later, as we headed towards the tarn, making new friends and catching up with familiar faces, I felt so happy to be doing something positive for a good cause.

Shortly after the event, I arranged to meet Lee, the charity's head of operations for the region, who also serves as a GNAAS paramedic, so that we could hand over a cheque. In total, we'd raised over £40,000 to date and I wanted to stress that Paddy, Harry and I would continue to do everything we could to support them in honour of a lost friend.

Lee is such a great ambassador, as well as being very easy-going and excellent company. Paddy and Harry took an instant shine to him as we shook hands, which I always take as a good measure. We had a great chat about Max's Facebook page and how it had evolved over the years, while I continued to be that guy who asks lots of questions about working with helicopters. At the same time, I couldn't help but notice that Lee had arrived to meet me in a charity-branded sports utility car with emergency lights on the roof.

'That doesn't look much use in the air,' I observed, which earned a smile.

'It's our rapid response vehicle,' he told me and then went on to outline its importance to the charity's work.

In providing critical care at the scene, I learned that GNAAS relied on road transport when adverse conditions or mechanical breakdown prevented the choppers from flying. It enabled the charity to provide a 24-hour service across the region, but Lee didn't need to tell me that with just one car, resources were stretched.

'How do you manage?' I asked.

He considered the question for a moment.

'We do the best we can,' he assured me and then thanked me, Paddy and Harry once again for a donation that clearly meant so much to them.

'I'm sure we can help them do better,' I said to the dogs as we left.

22

Green Grass, Red Carpet

EVEN BEFORE THE LANDSCAPE TURNED from vibrant greens to the copper palette of autumn, I felt like it had been quite a year. Caring for Max in his final months and then preparing to say goodbye had been draining. Afterwards, time out with Paddy and Harry had helped me to recharge. It was so good to get back to long walks once again and to raise money for a good cause. From 'Paddy's Buttermere Bounce' to 'A Brew for Moo' – with an aerial spectacular surprise thrown in – it had all helped me build the confidence to be ambitious. I always wanted our events to bring Max's community together – that simple goal had to be at the heart of it all – but I felt that with Paddy and Harry, we could raise our game in terms of our fundraising target.

In view of what I had learned about GNAAS and their work, there could only be one goal. If we could raise enough money to gift a second rapid response vehicle, that would be a fitting legacy for a dog who gave so much. It was a tall order, especially when I set myself the target of raising enough money by the end of that year. As the pledges to the sponsored walks kept climbing beyond my expectation, as well as the numbers joining us, I believed that we could do it. Max's online community were so generous at heart and I felt sure they would get behind a vital cause such as this.

'Picture this,' I said one morning at The Paw Store. The idea had come to my mind as I worked. When I turned to share it with the dogs, both Paddy and Harry sat up and cocked their heads. 'A Christmas show for Max's online community with you guys in the lead roles ...' Harry responded with an anxious whine. Paddy simply dropped his head back on his front paws. 'Don't worry,' I added, 'I'll be sharing the stage with you. After everything we've been through, we can bring everyone together for a year in review that raises funds for our favourite charity.'

Now, I had their full attention. This was largely down to the fact that I'd plucked two treats from a bag as I made my pitch. Even so, I felt sure that Paddy and Harry would share the spotlight, even if the prospect seemed frankly terrifying to me at the time. By now I had grown used to public speaking, but hosting an entire show would no doubt bring another level of anxiety. I envisaged a kind of one-man, two-dog show in which we remembered Max, honoured his passing but also celebrated the good times we'd shared with Harry and Paddy over the previous twelve months. We'd relive the walks, the fundraising events, the triumphs and mishaps. It would be fun, I hoped, with plenty of smiles as well as tears. Also, I couldn't ignore the fact that it would be a huge responsibility and if I failed to deliver then people would talk about the event for all the wrong reasons. I just had to remind myself that it was Max who first helped me to find the courage to reclaim my life. Even though he'd gone, I knew he'd be watching over us when the curtain went up.

From that moment on, I began to plan. Above all, I wanted to do this as a way of celebrating Max in a happy light. We had been through so much sadness, which is only natural when losing a loved one, but I didn't want to lose sight of the fact that he'd been such a positive force. I felt we owed him a celebration, while at the same time recognising that both Paddy and Harry were continuing his good work. Aiming high, I set my sights on staging the event at a landmark building in Keswick. The Old Pencil Factory was built in 1916 by the Cumberland Pencil Company. It's a handsome white building, with big windows overlooking a bow in the River Greta, that serves today as a venue for conferences and exhibitions. As soon as I booked it for the week before Christmas, having first toured the space, I set about worrying that I'd been too ambitious. *What if only a dozen people showed up?* I asked myself. *People would have plans, after all.* I had purposely picked the festive season because as a kid I used to have a miserable experience. I didn't get on with my stepfather and somehow it had felt like his treatment of me during the holiday was unusually cruel and heartless. From the upswing in visitors to Max's Facebook page over that period, I knew that I wasn't alone in finding it tough. I thought the event would be an opportunity to have fun and help everyone to feel part of a community but I was also well aware that for the vast majority, Christmas was a wonderful time of year. *What if nobody comes at all?*

As I started to plan content for the show, I received an invitation that made me feel like perhaps this was a worthwhile venture after all. It was a great honour to learn that together with Paddy and Harry, and in memory of Max, we had won a nomination for Fundraiser of the Year from the prestigious Pride of Britain Awards. This annual event recognises efforts by ordinary people who have acted bravely or extraordinarily in challenging situations. We had been put forward for our fundraising efforts, particularly during lockdown. It came as a tremendous surprise and one that made me feel as if we hadn't done as much as others to deserve such an amazing nomination. Quite simply, I feel very fortunate to be in the company of such amazing dogs that can inspire people to do good things. I'm also very lucky to live in such a beautiful part of the world that makes a simple walk such a huge pleasure. It was easy to share the experience by livestream and so rewarding to know that it helped people in all sorts of different ways. That it also inspired Max's online community to come together and support others was the icing on the cake and so we prepared to attend the awards ceremony on their behalf.

The last time Angela and I travelled to London, we had escorted Max when he was invited to attend the Buckingham Palace Garden Party. Paddy and Harry had stayed behind with friends. They were in great hands, but I still didn't like leaving them. Now it felt like their time had come – they were the real heroes here, after all, and I wanted them to enjoy the recognition. Personally, I didn't relish the prospect of leaving the Lake District. Visiting London is an amazing experience, but I could never feel settled so far from home and in such an urban environment. Even just booking trains and a hotel made me feel anxious and so it was a blessing to know that I would have both Angela and the dogs for company.

'So, this is the capital,' I said to Paddy and Harry, on their first ever journey south by rail as the train pulled into the station. 'There are no sheep here, but I will have to keep you both on leads.'

The dogs had been at the carriage window, watching with interest as the landscape outside became increasingly defined by buildings rather than open spaces.

'It must be so strange for them,' Angela observed.

'They're not alone,' I said and braced myself to make the most of this visit.

That evening, having rested in our hotel, we set out by black cab for the ceremony. Angela looked very elegant and the boys scrubbed up smartly in their harnesses. I had chosen orange for them both as a way to remember Max, while I wore a tie to match. Even so, in my suit I couldn't help but feel as if I was dressed for my first job interview. When the cab pulled up outside Grosvenor House in Mayfair, in front of a red carpet flanked by photographers, I sensed my heart move into my mouth.

'How exciting,' said Angela, while I clung to Harry and Paddy as if we were in deep water and I needed them to keep me afloat.

Without their presence, I would have asked the driver to take me back to the hotel. With the dogs leading the way, however, I reminded myself that I was simply the support act and then smiled with my wife for the cameras.

Mr Irving, over here! This way, Kerry! Smile!

As the paparazzi flashes went off, I was dazzled in more ways than one. All of a sudden, we were the centre of attention and I felt light years from home. I faced the photographers with Angela as requested and then knelt down with Paddy and Harry so all three of us could fit in the frame. The celebrity food writer and presenter, Mary Berry, had arrived at the same time and I stood in disbelief as she made a fuss of the dogs. Then the boxing legend, Frank Bruno, made his entrance and stopped to compliment me on how well behaved they were. They were both so charming, yet I felt completely over-whelmed. It was only when my eyes adjusted that I took in the crowds that had come to see the guests arriving. That's when I spotted a scattering of orange bobble hats with Max's signature patch and it felt like I was among friends.

'Thank you so much for coming,' I said, having stopped to talk to everyone who had ventured out to see Paddy and Harry. 'It really does mean a great deal.'

Inside the main hall, my first task was to settle Paddy and Harry under our table. I was well aware that it wasn't just me who was faced with an unfamiliar environment and yet they remained so calm and compliant throughout. It helped that when food was served the dogs were on hand to catch anything dropped by those who shared our table, either by accident or on purpose, and I certainly kept them busy with a steady offering of beef from the main course. It meant they were sound asleep by the time the presentations began.

I was in awe of all the incredible individuals and groups who had been nominated for awards. There were guys who had rowed across the Atlantic for a cause, youngsters who had defied their disabilities for charity and police officers who showed incredible bravery during the course of their duties. The people of Ukraine were also honoured for their courage and poise in the face of unspeakable aggression. These people were all deserving winners. It was so good to see them collect their awards on stage and I was just happy that we'd made it as far as the shortlist. I was also very glad that I had overcome my reluctance to come to London for it was an opportunity to see people at their very best.

*　　*　　*

Despite being a long way from home, the next morning I stirred at my usual early hour. Paddy and Harry were already awake when I padded out of bed to check on them and so having dressed, we crept out of the hotel to stretch our legs. We were staying close to the South Bank. Within a minute we were strolling along beside the River Thames. With the moon still presiding over the high-rise rooftops and its reflection shimmering on the water, the city took on a whole new complexion. It wasn't deserted, but I appreciated the peace. If anything, it reminded me just what I was missing back in Keswick. Paddy and Harry also seemed grateful when I unclipped them from their leads so they could roam. They stayed close by, content to take in their surroundings at my leisurely pace. Approaching the London Eye, which looked magnificent lit up against the night sky, I paused to absorb the moment. We were standing at the edge of Jubilee Gardens and it was nice to feel close to trees and greenery once more. I was so lost in thought about the contrasting draw of city and countryside that I failed to notice the security guard approaching me.

'Excuse me, sir,' he said. 'You'll need to keep your dogs on a lead here.'

'Oh, of course!' I said, as if stirring from a dream, and immediately called Paddy and Harry to heel.

'No problem,' he said as they trotted back to say hello to my new friend. 'Are they Springer Spaniels?'

As he chatted, I detected a South African accent, which transported me back to my earliest childhood years when my family lived in Cape Town. I'm always keen to reminisce whenever I have the chance and we talked about life in the country for several minutes under the streetlamps.

'It was good to meet you,' I said finally as the guard gave the dogs one final pat before continuing with his patrol. It had only been a short conversation, but it reminded me that even in a city of millions, it only took one nice individual to make a difference.

'Enjoy your visit, sir,' he said on turning to leave, only to pause and come around full circle. 'And you can leave the dogs off the lead,' he added with a grin. 'Let them play.'

*   *   *

We had booked a taxi to take us from the hotel to the train station. It was due to arrive at eight that morning, giving us plenty of time to catch our train an hour later. Ten minutes after it was due to show up, I grew nervous. At half past eight, I was pacing in front of the pick-up point while Angela wondered out loud if we could travel with our case and two dogs by Underground. I really didn't want to put Paddy and Harry through that ordeal, however. Especially not at rush hour. I wasn't even sure that I could cope with it myself.

'He'll be here,' I said through gritted teeth.

Hailing another taxi wasn't an option. With the dogs in tow I knew they'd drive on by, which is why I had made this special reservation with a pet-friendly cab company. Whose phone was constantly engaged when I called them repeatedly.

Finally, with no time to spare, the taxi fishtailed into the pick-up point.

'I'm so sorry, guys,' said the driver as he rushed out to help us with our cases. 'They sent me to the wrong hotel!'

I was too busy bundling the dogs into the back seat to reply. Once Angela was safely inside and I had squeezed in alongside her, I shut the door and instructed him to drive.

'We've got to catch this train!' I declared, as if we had to get home at all costs.

The traffic was horrendous. Our driver mined his knowledge of the roads to take every short-cut that he knew, only to barrel into crawling traffic and even grid-lock. Angela and I each had a dog on our lap. Paddy and Harry seemed to love the thrill of the chase from the back seat and so when we finally raced into the drop-off area outside the station, they were ready to leap into action.

'Spaniels coming through!'

With tickets in hand, and less than a minute to spare, we sprinted for the platform where our train was preparing to leave. It must have been quite a sight to see this couple steering baggage and two dogs in orange harnesses across the concourse. Indeed, several people called out, having recognised Paddy and Harry.

'I'm so sorry but we can't stop,' I said, panting hard. *'Hold that train!'*

We jumped aboard with a moment to spare, collapsing into our seats as if we'd just run a marathon.

'Well, that was an experience!' said Angela eventually.

'Never to be repeated,' I replied, having checked to see both dogs were settled under our table. 'You can lose me in the mountains and I'd survive,' I added. 'In London, I wouldn't know where to begin.'

'At least we're heading in the right direction now,' she said, laughing.

'It's one way for me,' I told her. 'I've had a fantastic time, but give me green grass over red carpets any time.'

23

Wide Stick, Narrow Gate

SOMETIMES, OUR COURSE THROUGH LIFE changes without warning. It can create all manner of challenges, as I discovered for myself when living with chronic pain all those years ago, and also open pathways that bring out the very best in us. I had Max to thank for showing me how to reclaim my future. Others rely on guardian angels in different guises.

When Ava was just two years old, she was involved in a terrible road accident. Having suffered life-threatening injuries, the little girl was treated at the scene by GNAAS paramedics and air-lifted to hospital. Without their swift action, she would have died. Thanks to the rapid response provided by the team and her incredible fighting spirit throughout years of recovery and rehabilitation, she's gone on to become a fantastic ambassador for the charity and an example to us all.

I first met Ava, aged nine, along with her wonderful mother, Amy, early in my relationship with GNAAS. After everything she had suffered, she was such an impressive young lady. She also loved dogs, especially Paddy and Harry, and so I felt it would be fitting to invite her to take part in our end-of-year show. By then, I had decided to call it *A Christmas Tail*, with all proceeds from the evening going to the charity. I had also involved GNAAS from the start, simply because I wanted people to hear about their work. I knew it would appeal to the kind hearts and generosity of Max's online community and hoped that Lee might speak on their behalf. In case he needed someone there to provide support and inspiration, I was delighted to confirm that Ava would be joining us.

'Would it be OK if I introduced you to our audience?' I asked her when she and Amy popped over for a visit. Having joined us at several events, they had become good friends.

Ava regarded me like she needed to have a long, hard think about that question.

'Of course!' she declared breezily. 'Will the dogs be with me?'

'From start to finish,' I assured her.

*　　*　　*

Despite my ongoing anxiety about whether anyone would turn up, I was comfortable with planning a big event. Our fundraising walks had grown from a few dozen attendees to hundreds of people from all around the world. So many had joined us that summer for 'A

Brew for Moo' that I'd purposely had to choose a start and finish location with adequate parking. We encouraged people to lift share or use public transport in a bid to minimise our carbon footprint. It was great to see so many act upon that, but the sheer numbers meant it was an operation that required a great deal of forward thinking. It involved time and patience, not just from me but Paddy and Harry, and we loved it. Max would have been in his element, too, and that became a motivating force.

'That's a nice picture of him. Wide stick. Narrow gate. Classic Max! What do you think, boys?'

It took me a great deal of time to select photographs for the show. I planned to give a talk with the two dogs at my feet and a projector with a screen behind me to keep everyone entertained. Paddy and Harry inspected each image I showed them on my laptop, but ultimately, I went with my gut instinct. As an amateur photographer, my pet subject was capturing moments with my dogs out on the fells. With the dramatic landscape of the Lake District as a backdrop, I loved to celebrate the sense of freedom that my spaniels knew how to enjoy. It was also brilliant to see Angela had grown so passionate about working with a camera. Her pictures could be breathtaking and so I was spoiled for choice.

Thanks to GNAAS, I also had a short film to include that I simply couldn't watch without tears in my eyes. It was basically a montage of their work through the year, which included shots of our Max, as well as Paddy and

Harry with the helicopter when it joined us for 'A Brew for Moo'. The whole package was underscored by 'Heroes', the classic song by David Bowie and an absolute favourite of mine. The film was beautifully made and I couldn't wait to share this gem on the night. I had the charity's chief fundraiser, Hannah, to thank for providing it. In the early stages of my planning for the show I had reached out to her – I wanted the charity to be involved and for her to know that every penny raised would be dedicated to supporting their work.

I also had a proposition for her and a small secret I needed her to keep.

'On behalf of Max's online community,' I told Hannah when we met to discuss the project, 'we'd like to raise the funds to provide you with a second emergency support vehicle.'

Hannah had looked to Paddy and Harry as if to check if I was joking. They didn't blink, but wagged their tails when she stroked them.

'Well, that would be quite a Christmas present,' she said eventually.

'On one condition,' I added playfully. 'Can we keep it from Lee and the crew? We were thinking it would make a lovely surprise.'

*   *   *

Raising the funds for a new GNAAS emergency support vehicle was ambitious, but we were already on the road to meeting our target. Support for our ventures had grown so big that 'Paddy's Buttermere Bounce' raised £42,000 alone, followed by £36,000 for 'A Brew for Moo', and Hannah had agreed to ring-fence that money. We needed just under £100,000 to secure the emergency response vehicle. It required all kinds of specialist fittings and so it needed to be commissioned in good time. We still had a long way to go, however, and so Paddy, Harry and I made every effort to appeal to the generous nature of Max's online community. Ultimately, I wanted to make this festive season one to remember for the paramedics who provided such a vital service across the region.

With both the date and the stage set, and also a loose script to follow, I had just one other obstacle left to overcome: my nerves. In recent years I had carried out plenty of public speaking, thanks to the invitations from schools and workplaces to bring in the dogs and talk about the mental and physical benefits of getting outdoors. This seemed different somehow – there was such a lot riding on it. At first, I made 700 seats available. The Pencil Factory could easily accommodate that number; the hall I had booked was really just a big open space. I was simply trying to put a realistic figure on the likely number of people who would attend. When those tickets were snapped up online, I increased the number to 900. After they went in a heartbeat too, I capped it at 1,200. I couldn't even picture that many people in an audience – I was also mindful that I needed to set out chairs for everyone!

'You might have to learn a new trick,' I suggested to Paddy and Harry as I posted an update to say that the event was sold out.

I had decided to make it a free event as a means of thanking everyone for all their support over the years. People had been so kind and generous and this would be our way of giving back. I was also mindful of those who often reached out to me as they were unable to join our group rambles for various reasons. Some struggled with anxiety and worried about having to walk and talk, while others lived with mobility issues. As a result, I really wanted this to be an evening that would cater for everyone. With a fundraising page to run alongside the event, I hoped we would meet our target in time so that we could finish the evening in a way that would be remembered for a long time to come.

* * *

As I watched the total figure rise through autumn and into winter, along with the pressure I had placed myself under, I found myself having long, hard chats with Paddy and Harry on our walks.

'Can we talk about how you guys stay so calm and relaxed on stage? I just want to be myself and address the audience like old friends.'

They never provided me with an answer, of course, but in putting my worries into words I found some perspective. So what if I stumbled over a line or two? As long as I put my heart and soul into the performance, the real stars of the show would be at my side from start to finish. When I looked at it like this, and with thanks to my four-legged counsellors, I found myself looking forward to putting on the best show possible.

Thanks to Max, Paddy and Harry, I have come to understand what makes me tick. I like the great outdoors and time with my dogs. I'm dependable, trustworthy, easily enthused in the name of a great cause; I also hope I can be good company but one thing I'm not is a natural performer. I'm an introvert at heart and there's nothing wrong with that. While I love to meet people and make new friends, that's a world away from facing into the glare of stage lights and delivering a performance designed to transport an audience for over an hour. In particular, I can become quite emotional when talking about things I care about. As Max would be at the heart of the show, I was seriously worried about whether I would get through it.

It was something I pondered for quite a while until I looked at Paddy and Harry and realised that I should just be myself. Both dogs have distinct personalities, from Paddy's swaggering boldness to the sensitive, caring character that has come to define Harry. That's just who they are, in any situation, and I figured I should follow their example on stage. So, if I became emotional at times, I wouldn't try to hide it. People know I wear my heart on my sleeve and I really wanted this show to feel authentic. It all came down to a passion for dogs, which isn't something unique to me. It's a bond that speaks to so many of us and I intended for that to resonate from start to finish.

*   *   *

As we approached December, what had become the central plank of my preparations finally fell into place.

'We've done it!' I said out loud on checking the fundraising page and got straight on the phone to Hannah at GNAAS so that we could get things underway. 'I'm calling about that car ...'

With the wheels in motion to have the emergency support vehicle ready as a surprise, I felt a huge sense of relief. It would still be a tight turnaround, but working with Hannah I felt sure that she would have it delivered on time. With just weeks to go, I found my working days were filled with juggling preparations for the event and fulfilling deliveries from The Paw Store. We were in the midst of calendar season once again. As much as I loved such positive feedback for producing something creative, the dogs and I were working long hours to package and post orders all around the world. It was that time of year when Paddy and Harry became familiar faces in the Post Office queue. Only this time, people approached to say how much they were looking forward to *A Christmas Tail*. The pressure was on, and without a doubt, I could not have carried it without my two precious spaniels. Having slipped their names onto the blocks supporting the plinth and Max's statue, I had since come to appreciate what support they also gave me.

I was determined to put on a show that celebrated Max's life, spirit and legacy and that was something I could only do with Paddy and Harry beside me. We were a team and committed to finishing this rollercoaster of a year on a high.

24
A Christmas Tail

THE PROBLEM WITH SURPRISE PRESENTS is that they need to be kept hidden until the big moment arrives. It's one thing when handling small items like jewellery, a book or a new phone, but quite another when it comes to a car.

'What are we going to do with it?' I asked out loud after the GNAAS emergency support vehicle had been delivered to The Paw Store. It was parked beside my van and frankly hard to ignore. Resplendent in the charity's green, white and yellow livery, and with a light bar mounted on the roof, it also sported an eye-catching GNAAS logo on the bonnet, along with lettering that spelled Critical Care Team. Paddy and Harry had ventured out to inspect the new arrival. I looked around nervously, expecting to see curtains twitching in the farmhouse. Keswick is a small town and word could spread like wildfire.

'Unless we find a hiding place, this could be the worst-kept secret ever!'

I was looking at Paddy when the idea came to mind to throw some plastic sheeting over the top of the car. Then I stopped to consider that it would basically draw attention to the fact that we had a vehicle to hide.

'That's not going to work,' I told him. 'Can you come up with a better suggestion?'

Harry had circled around to the bank overlooking the main road. He was just standing there, side on to the distant fells, gazing with purpose towards the town. No doubt he was just sniffing the air. Still, it drew my attention in the same direction and then led me to consider moving the car somewhere far from The Paw Store. Rather than head deeper into the hills, however, I fell upon the idea of hiding it in plain sight.

'Jump in, boys,' I said finally as a solution sprang to mind.

*   *   *

The car had arrived on the eve of the show. Winter had also swept in ahead of the big day, frosting the peaks around Keswick and encouraging everyone into coats, hats and scarves. With twinkling festive lights in every window and a huge tree on the high street, the town was ready for Christmas. I just couldn't see beyond the next day, which was set to be one of the biggest of my life.

Throughout the previous week, it had looked as if the emergency support vehicle might not be ready in time. The car required so many specialist fittings in order to be fit for purpose, which meant the slightest delay on a single aspect could scupper the event finale. Despite the pressure, Hannah did an amazing job in making sure the finished vehicle was delivered to my door. It was only then that I had considered what to do with it and panicked a little bit. For one thing, the car had been equipped with the very latest in life-saving technology. Quite simply, it was an incredibly expensive mobile trauma centre on wheels and there I was behind the wheel on icy roads. As I negotiated the road down into Keswick, I gripped the wheel tightly and placed all my faith in the brakes.

'Sit tight,' I told Paddy and Harry, who were watching me with interest from the back seat. 'And no shedding dog hair – the upholstery is brand new!'

I wanted the car to mark the grand finale of the show. Already I had been down to the Pencil Factory a few times to contemplate the hall. There, I'd identified a service entrance at the back of the hall with a big roller door. With careful choreography, I could drive the car in from behind the stage as a grand surprise for the audience as much as Lee and his fellow paramedics. I'd measured the width and it was tight. In fact, I had just two centimetres to play with on each side of the vehicle and that was enough to keep me lying awake at night. Paddy and Harry never complained about my driving, but the thought of steering the car cleanly through that gap gave me nightmares: one false move in front of a packed house and we'd be debuting an expensive vehicle in need of major body repair work.

Having reached the car park without incident, I was keen to get the vehicle inside the hall and out of sight. So, with help from the staff, I opened up the roller door and climbed back behind the wheel. By now, Paddy and Harry both picked up on the fact that I was about to do something risky. They were still in the back seat, but side by side in the middle so they had a clear view.

'All that's missing back there is a box of popcorn,' I grumbled, addressing them via the rear-view mirror. 'OK, hold tight. We're going in ...'

With a feather-like touch on the accelerator, I eased the car forward. I'd had to pull in the wing mirrors, but as we approached, I found myself breathing in as if somehow that would also help. With the car aligned as precisely as possible, I asked the dogs to wish me luck.

Upon which the car halted of its own accord.

'What the ...?' I pressed the pedal again gently as if fearing I might startle it, but the vehicle refused to respond. Aware that several staff members were watching me, as well as the dogs in the back, I smiled like I still had this under control. 'We've got this,' I said through gritted teeth.

I restarted the car, but it made no difference: the vehicle simply wouldn't move. This time, I shut off the engine, rifled through the delivery documents on the passenger seat and rang the customer support number.

Within the space of a minute, having spoken to a helpful lady who explained a key safety feature built into the car, I realised that I needed to find another entrance.

'It's the parking sensors,' I told my small audience of staff members and spaniels. 'Apparently I can override them with a stiff blip of the pedal, but frankly I don't fancy accelerating into an accident.'

*   *   *

That night, the emergency support vehicle stayed out in the Pencil Factory car park. I had left it in the most unassuming spot that I could find, behind the main building and out of sight from the riverbank. There were a few other cars dotted about so it didn't stand out as badly as it had, back at the farm. It was less than ideal but I had so much left to do in preparation for the show, time ran out on me. Before bed, I took Paddy and Harry for a final walk to clear my head. The last thing I wanted to do was finish the show by announcing a special surprise and then ask 1,200 people to file out into the elements to see it. There had to be a way to get the car inside and I resolved to crack it first thing in the morning.

A Christmas Tail was a collective effort. I could not have staged the entire show alone and was so thankful to all the volunteers who had answered my request for help on the day. We had stack upon stack of chairs to set out in the hall and refreshments to prepare, while I'd hired an audiovisual guy to cover the lighting and big screens. The show was due to start at one o'clock. By nine, Max's army had moved in to transform the hall. It was a hive of activity overseen by Paddy and Harry, who wandered freely and accepted all the attention they could find.

While the dogs were sources of calm and joy, I got stuck in, feeling my stress levels rising. I had arrived with the emergency support vehicle uppermost on my mind, only for that to become the least of my worries as the morning progressed. Overnight, the winter conditions had stiffened considerably. Having gained access to the hall, we discovered the water pipes supplying the taps in the kitchen had frozen. With tea and coffee to make for more than 1,000 people, we had a problem.

'The show is two hours long,' I said to anyone who would listen. 'How will anyone survive without a brew in the interval?'

While I felt like I was ageing in front of everyone, my lovely volunteers stayed calm and got creative. Within an hour, they had commandeered huge flagons and secured access to water from a neighbouring building. As I watched them shuttling back and forth to fill the urns, I wished that I could share their calm and poise. By the time Hannah arrived from GNAAS, ahead of Lee and his team, she found me staring at the only other possible entry point for the car. It was wider than the service entrance, but located to one side of the hall and right beside the stage. The gap was deep enough to accommodate the car – the trouble was that it would be in full view from the moment the audience took to their seats.

'Can't we cover it?' asked Hannah, inspecting the space.

'With what?' I asked. I peered up at a rail that would certainly allow us to hang something to hide the car. 'All I can find that's big enough is that tarpaulin.'

I gestured at the tatty, crumpled heap of plastic sheeting that I had dragged out from behind the stage. With no alternative at The Paw Store, and time running out, I glanced at Hannah and hoped she might have a better suggestion.

She didn't. In fact, what she had to say next made the situation a whole lot worse.

'I don't want to panic you, Kerry, but a lot of the main roads in the north are blocked by snow. Getting here has been a nightmare.'

I looked at my watch, barely able to breathe.

'But we start in just over an hour,' I said, in what sounded more like a whimper. 'What are we going to do?'

While my response was to pace the floor muttering to myself that we faced a disaster, Hannah took a firm grip of the situation. Having talked me into a temporary sense of calm, I recognised that our only option was to negotiate the emergency support vehicle into the hall through the side entrance by the stage and then hide it as best we could. With the car indoors at last, and with the help of the volunteers, we strung up the tarpaulin. It did the job intended, but was so long that we had to tuck the excess material under the front of the car. I tried hard not to picture myself making my entrance, only for the tarpaulin to snag and cloak the car, or pull down the hall's support beams with it. That Paddy was drawn to sniff the air also told me it probably smelled as bad as it looked.

'All the more reason for us to command audience attention until the big reveal,' I told him. 'We want all eyes on the stage.' I paused as Harry joined in with the inspection. 'That means you both have to shine brightly this afternoon ... that's if everyone isn't stuck in traffic.'

Under any other circumstances, I would have taken myself off for a walk with the dogs. It really is the best medicine for stress and anxiety. With little time left before the show started, and so many loose ends to tie off, I scurried around with everyone else in a bid to have everything ready. It was a collective effort and as people started to arrive, I was relieved as well as hugely grateful.

'We're up to double figures,' I told Hannah. 'At least the hall won't be completely empty.'

'They'll come,' she said with absolute certainty.

It was a relief to see Lee and his team arrive. I couldn't resist asking if they'd flown in, but had to force myself to hide my excitement at the surprise we had in store for them. Paddy and Harry were equally pleased to see them – I just hoped they wouldn't want to share their enthusiasm for the tarpaulin. Thanks to some stage light trickery, it hung there in the shadows without drawing attention to the fact that it was hiding something very special.

When Ava arrived, along with her mum, Amy, I wished that I shared her boundless confidence. She breezed in and showed me the bookmarks she had made to raise money for GNAAS.

'Those are beautiful,' I told her.

'They're two pounds each!' she said, 'but when people give me five- and ten-pound notes, I just put the change in the charity pot.'

My smile froze momentarily. I glanced at her mother, who shrugged like Ava called the shots.

'And I'm sure you'll sell them all,' I told her, before reminding her that I intended to introduce her to the audience from the stage. She just nodded like it was no big deal, which made it quite clear to me that I would be in the supporting role.

'I hope I can be as cool as Ava one day,' I told Amy, who chuckled at her daughter's confidence. 'Right now, I'm looking at a half-empty hall and trying hard not to panic!'

* * *

Heading into the last half-hour before the show was due to start, I could have cried as the seats began to fill. So many guests arrived wearing orange, which was lovely, and with well-behaved dogs welcomed, it was great to hear a few barks in among the chatter. As I helped guide people to their seats, I heard shocking stories of the queues they'd been forced to endure on winter roads. As the bad weather had been forecast, however, most had set off early to allow extra time. I had thought we might have to delay proceedings. It was only as the last arrivals settled into the remaining chairs that it dawned on me what would happen next.

'That's it,' I whispered to Angela. I had joined her in the wings, where Paddy and Harry were waiting patiently with her. Having been present in the hall since we started setting up, they were completely unfazed by the rising sense of expectation. 'I've got no choice now, I'll have to start the show!'

'You can do it,' she said calmly, which is what I needed to hear. 'The dogs will be with you – Max, too,' she added with a smile.

Just hearing his name helped bring me to my senses. I reminded myself to breathe slowly. Yes, this was the biggest speaking engagement I'd ever undertaken, but despite the scale, I wasn't concerned about stepping up in front of so many people. Given the story I wanted to share, I doubted I could hold onto my emotions and that still rattled me somewhat. I had no script to hand, or lines I needed to remember. In my mind, I had marked out waypoints through the story of our final year with the world's most-loved dog. With that, I planned to speak from the heart. As I stepped up onto the stage, I hoped that the joy, happiness and tears I had experienced would connect with everyone.

With Paddy and Harry at my side, the chatter in the hall fell away. I peered out into the audience, momentarily dazzled by the theatre lights. Harry looked up at me, brushing my side as he did so, which was my cue to begin.

'If you're hoping that I'm going to introduce you to a new puppy,' I began and paused for the collective intake of breath, 'prepare to be disappointed ...'

I had hoped to start with the laugh that followed; I also wanted to address what was shaping up to be an elephant in the room. Throughout the autumn and into the winter, everyone had asked me if I'd be bringing a new spaniel into the mix. I loved puppies, but my mind was as made up as it had been when I decided to pass on one of Bella and Paddy's paellas. Even though Max had passed away in that time, I was worried about the dynamics of bringing another dog into the mix. He had always walked beside me, while Paddy was off doing Paddy things. Now Harry had taken that role at my side, but in some ways we were still finding our feet. And so it was as a trio that we kicked off proceedings with a special little film that I hoped would strike all the right chords. As the opening bars of David Bowie's 'Heroes' reached out across the hall, I took the dogs to one side and let the montage of pictures and clips introduce an eventful year. I could barely bring myself to watch and when I saw members of the audience dabbing at their eyes, I had to look at the floor.

'Hold it together,' I muttered under my breath because from the moment the film finished, I had a tale to tell.

Paddy and Harry remained so calm. I reached down to ruffle their ears in turn, as if drawing confidence from them, before registering the music fade and stepping forward into the spotlight.

'Welcome, everyone, to A Christmas Tail ...'

*   *   *

Over the course of the next two hours, sharing the stage with Paddy and Harry, I felt Max's presence throughout. He was there among us as I shared our story and I hope we made him proud as I introduced Ava to the audience. Her in-built confidence didn't waver in front of so many people. In fact, when she took the microphone that little girl commanded anyone who hadn't bought a bookmark to do so before her stock ran out. With plenty of questions and answers in the mix, and such a supportive atmosphere throughout, I found the experience to be great fun and also cathartic. There were times when I addressed moments in our year that caused a catch in my throat. Sometimes I even needed a moment to steady my composure, but that was fine. Even though I'd never met most of the people who had come out to share the afternoon with me, I felt that I was among friends.

With the show dedicated to GNAAS, it was an honour to invite Lee onto the stage. He received a huge round of applause and it was a pleasure to bring people up to present cheques for sums they had raised themselves for the charity. Having worked so closely with GNAAS over the year, it felt like it sealed a lasting relationship. The charity had already made Max, Paddy and Harry honorary crew members and the photos we shared to mark the occasion were priceless. I also wanted the audience to hear first-hand what vital work these guys did for us and they listened closely to every story that Lee shared. Then, in taking questions about the charity's fantastic work, I steered the conversation towards the importance of their sole emergency support vehicle.

'What would be the dream?' I asked Lee at one point.

At the time, a picture of their only road vehicle filled the screen.

'Another car would help us grow towards reaching everyone who needs us,' he said, turning to face the image of the car. 'Maybe in time it will happen.'

'Well, Max was there for me when I needed him,' I said. 'That kind of commitment saves lives. He taught me that helping others is such a gift. Speaking of which, Lee, we have a little Christmas present for you …'

It was here that I brought Angela on to the stage. I really felt she deserved recognition for all the support she had shown throughout the years. As she was someone who had always preferred to stay in the wings, I was so proud to see her receive a standing ovation.

'So, did you bring it?' I asked, having planned this moment with her.

'Bring what?'

'Lee's present.'

'Oh,' said Angela, feigning surprise. 'I thought you were going to take care of it?'

If we had hoped to create a moment of drama and uncertainty, it worked wonders. Leaving Lee and Angela under the spotlight, I asked Paddy and Harry to follow me. Together, we walked into the wings, marching towards the tatty tarpaulin we had hung from the roof beam. I grumbled to myself at the same time, trying hard not to laugh as Hannah waited to help me with the next step. As soon as I ducked behind the cover hiding the car, I opened the passenger door for the dogs to hop on board. Then, having whisked around to jump behind the wheel, I fired up the engine and activated the blue flashing lights. It was the cue that Hannah had been waiting for. As I shifted into gear, she pulled the tarpaulin clear and I swung Lee's gleaming surprise into the hall.

'Look at his face,' I remarked to Paddy and Harry as we steered the car into the space between the stage and the audience. 'What a picture!'

Together with the dogs, I climbed out to wild cheers, whoops and applause. Poor Lee was overwhelmed. The unveiling had gone perfectly and yet as the clapping subsided, I had one final surprise in store.

'Ava,' I said, and gestured for my premium-priced bookmark seller to join us once again. 'There's something I'd like you to do for me.'

The new emergency support vehicle was sparkling under the theatre lights. It looked incredible with the blue lamps revolving and yet when I walked the little girl around to the rear of the car, I drew everyone's attention to the fact that three small areas of the bodywork at the back and the sides were covered with paper and tape.

'Should I?' said Ava and stopped there when I nodded.

At the start of the year, we had made another little girl's day by presenting her with a bike. The frame proudly bore a sticker that declared it was Powered by Max. Complete with his pawprint, it had always struck me as a powerful and inspiring stamp to those he had helped throughout his life. And as Ava revealed that the car shared the same endorsement, from a dog who meant so much to so many, I witnessed almost everyone in that hall – including me – melt into tears.

'Happy Christmas, one and all!' I declared to yet more applause from the audience and then barking from the canine contingency. Then I turned to Lee. We shook hands but that quickly turned to a wholehearted hug while Paddy and Harry circled us happily, tails wagging. After such a year of raw emotion, I couldn't have wished for any other ending. 'This is from all of us,' I said, handing him the keys, 'but above all, it's with love from Max.'

EPILOGUE

Max was one of a kind. He saved my life, pure and simple. Nothing could replace him. I knew that from the moment we said goodbye in a pocket of woodland by the lake that he always loved so much. Max was my best friend and confidante. He was a listener, with unquestioning loyalty and so much love to share. I felt blessed that he became such an inspiration not just to me but to hundreds of thousands of people all around the world. Together with Paddy and Harry, their fund-raising ventures continue to leave me overwhelmed. It's not just a measure of their characters, and what they represent to those in need of a little ray of hope in their lives, but also the boundless generosity of Max's online community. To date, I am so proud to say that we have raised almost £800,000 for good causes and that began when I came across a lonely dog in a yard who showed me that life is there to be embraced and celebrated.

So, when Max went to sleep for a final time a chapter closed. I still look back knowing we did the very best for him when he needed us and that will always bring me comfort. Of course, I still had Paddy and Harry, and those two characters support me as they once did for Max. Over time, we have grown to accept that he has gone and yet I see him in different ways now. From a sapling tree in Memory Wood, drawing in wildlife as it grows beneath a Cumbrian sky to a hazy orange sunrise on our morning walks, Max is there in every pledge we receive for a charity walk and in the smiles of those who have felt so lost and alone when they find companionship in dogs. Yes, we miss him hugely, but he's always in my heart.

Ultimately, Max showed me how to wake up each morning and set out to make the most of the day. Happiness, contentment and purpose is something we can all find within ourselves and for me that came down to sharing my life with spaniels.

Which is how I found myself preparing to meet a new member of the Brown-Legged Gang.

Yes, I know what I had said in opening *A Christmas Tail* and at the time I meant every word. Then we moved into a new year, leaving behind one filled with so much emotion. There, I had the space and clarity of thought to review where I had been, where I was and where I was heading.

'Well, hello!' I said as an excitable little lady trotted out to greet me. As soon as I reached down to ruffle her ear, this doe-eyed Springer Spaniel was on her back, begging for a belly rub. 'Oh, it's like that! OK, if this is how we're greeting each other then I'm Kerry. Pleased to meet you!'

After Max, I didn't feel the time was right for another dog. I couldn't replace him, nor did I want to. But as Paddy, Harry and I reshaped our dynamic in his absence and a new season dawned with spring, I came to recognise that we could bring a new personality into the mix. It came down to continuation, something that meant so much to me when Paddy and Bella had puppies. Since they came into the world, I have loved seeing little Furgus grow into the fine adult dog that he is today. He has shades of his father's swagger, while his sisters, Mabel and Cora, share their mother's sweet gaze. I'm so pleased that as friends with their owners we've become one big spaniel family. The connection they share is something very special, with each other as well as their owners. Adam and Lisa also have children and it's so lovely to see them grow up with their four-legged friends. That continuation bonds genera-tions of dogs and humans, and that's how I came to realise that I had the time, commitment and energy to bring another Springer into our lives. It wouldn't be a replacement for Max, but one that could work with Paddy and Harry to inspire others, provide support and a sense of hope, raise funds for great causes and keep building his legacy.

Having made the decision, I found myself travelling to Scotland once more. There, a good friend owned a fantastic Springer Spaniel, who had recently given birth to a litter of puppies. The dog had come out to greet me when I visited, in fact, and bewitched me within moments.

'So, where are your pups?' I asked as she squirmed happily with all the attention I was giving her. She fixed her playful eyes on me, tongue lolling, like she'd momentarily forgotten all about her brood. 'I guess you're enjoying the break, right?'

Before I made the journey, the owner had told me that one boy in particular from the litter had tan markings on its face that would remind me of someone special. She shared clips with me and that was all I needed to see. I couldn't wait to meet the little guy and looked up at the garden gate through which his mother had just appeared.

As I did so, a pattering sound took shape from the yard beyond. It was quickly accompanied by yelps and squeaks that built in volume and urgency. Within seconds, the noise had become a low-level stampede.

'Oh,' I said to myself and slowly rose to my feet.

Sensing her attention was over, and aware of what was coming, the mother flipped back onto her paws and crept away. Upon which the narrow space behind the open gate filled with a tidal wave of puppies. Before I could take a step back, they were scrambling over each other in their bid to reach me, leaving little stripes of wee on the flagstones behind them, and when the pups hit me, I just submitted. There were eight of them in total, but combined they possessed the energy and enthusiasm of eighty. On my knees, I found myself entirely surrounded. Some tried to scramble up my back and arms, while one practically winded me by landing squarely on my lap. With great boldness, he then planted his front paws on my chest and reached up to lick my chin. I reached out to steady him and in that moment saw a marking on the pup's back that looked remarkably like a letter 'M'. Not only that but the fact that one side of his hind quarters was tan meant that I knew he'd fit right in.

'Looks like he's found you,' said my friend, who had appeared at the gate. 'I knew you'd be perfect for each other.'

'He's ... a lot,' I said as the pup continued to wash my face. 'But lovely.'

My friend laughed, reaching out to pet the pups' mum, who had joined her at the gate.

'He'll find his place with Paddy and Harry,' she said. 'Rest assured, things will never be the same again.'

'I sense that,' I said as the litter attempted to drag me down. By now, the pup who had claimed me as his own was halfway to gaining a foothold on my face. Every time I caught sight of his eyes, I saw a look of sheer devotion even though we'd only just met. Wisely, Paddy and Harry had stayed in the van. In time, I would introduce them once everyone calmed down, even if that looked like it was going to take quite a while. All I knew was this little guy looked set to shake up our lives no end.

'Do you have a name for him?' my friend asked.

'It'll come,' I said, 'when he gives me the personal space to think of something.'

I glanced at my friend as she chuckled, thanked her for thinking of me and then joked about a cooling-off period. We both laughed at that, though I had no intention of walking away now. We were in this together, just as I had been when a dog called Max sought my attention when I was in despair and then expanded the boundaries of my world.

'Hand on heart,' I said while wrestling with this ball of infinite affection in my arms, 'I'm looking forward to seeing where this one takes us.'

ACKNOWLEDGEMENTS

I want to thank everyone who showed us so much love and compassion when we lost Max. Both Angela and I were overwhelmed by the outpouring of emotion and support from across the globe, together with our amazing friends who checked in on us daily after Max's passing: a heartfelt thank you to you all.

To everyone who supported our walks and helped raise funds for the Great North Air Ambulance Service, you have been outstanding. Max saved and changed lives while he was living and continues to do so now in his legacy. Through supporting this amazing charity, Max continues to make a difference, so thank you, one and all. A special thank you to Hannah and the team at GNAAS for supporting our events.

We can all be #PoweredbyMax

I have met so many incredible and inspiring people thanks to Max. I've listened to individuals from all walks of life talk about their own personal journeys; some have been filled with happiness, others steeped in tragedy, filled with grief and loss. I thank every one of you for your bravery in taking that first step forward, sharing your stories of how Max, Paddy and Harry have helped you through the daily obstacles. Dogs just make our lives better.

To Charlotte and Holly, you are so brave, you will both go on to do great things. Harry S, you inspire me – it was a privilege to meet you all and plant trees together and talk. I will always look at Cherry Trees and think of your beautiful sister, Emily. You all have a very special place in my heart.

Amanda, I will always be indebted to your veterinary professionalism, the care, compassion, dignity and love you gave Max in his final days, and you continue to do so with Paddy and Harry. You are an absolute star. A thank you does not really repay what you gave us and our online community.

The incredible people at HarperCollins yet again for your ongoing support and belief in bringing this amazing team together again. Thank you all so much for all that you do.

Matt Whyman, I look on you as a friend. You've put together my jumbled words once again to create another three years of my life beautifully. I'm forever in your debt.

**If you're feeling sad, lonely or in need of a friend, look
to the sunset. Look for the orange, think of Max, the
little dog with the biggest heart and the waggiest of
tails, and he'll be there for you.**

Thank you, Moo, for all that you do.